The Harried Leisure Class

THE HARRIED
LEISURE CLASS

BY

Staffan Burenstam Linder

COLUMBIA UNIVERSITY PRESS

New York

Copyright © 1970 Columbia University Press
International Standard Book Number: 0-231-08649-0 *Paperbound*
International Standard Book Number: 0-231-03302-8 *Clothbound*
Printed in the United States of America
10 9 8 7 6 5 4

To My Children
Mariana and Göran

The ideas presented in this book stemmed initially from a short and little noticed paper written by Roy F. Harrod in 1958. On the theme of an increasing scarcity of time, I then wrote a short essay that was published in 1963. Active work on the present book was started toward the end of 1964. Concentrated writing was made possible by a generous offer to spend a number of months at the Economic Growth Center of Yale University during the autumn of 1966.

In order that I might enjoy the benefit of my colleagues' criticism, I originally wrote this book in English. With a view to reducing the lack of clarity in the argument and its presentation, I wrote the final version of the manuscript in Swedish. Mr. Keith Bradfield has helped me carry the text back into English.

Among those from whose advice and opinions I have benefited, I should like particularly to mention Stephen Hymer, Fred L. Pryor, and Clark W. Reynolds, all of whom were working at the Economic Growth Center while I was there. Gary S. Becker and Victor R. Fuchs read and commented upon my manuscript at a later stage.

The Swedish Council for Social Science Research has given me grants for the procurement of certain literature and to meet translation costs. Stockholms Enskilda Bank has also supported my work in various ways.

K.–G. Mäler has placed his mathematical knowledge at my disposal and has been of great assistance in my efforts to formalize the central arguments in a mathematical appendix. The library of the Stockholm School of Economics and, in particular, Miss Margareta Lundén there have been of great service in obtaining literature of a type different from that usually handled by the library. Mrs. Kerstin Johanson has checked the references and quotations. Miss Brita Modin has been mainly responsible for the onerous task of typing numerous versions of the manuscript.

To all these persons and institutions I would express my heartfelt thanks.

S. B. L.

Contents

*Till now man has been up against Nature;
from now on he will be up against his own nature.*

DENNIS GABOR, *Inventing the Future*

CHAPTER I

The Increasing Scarcity of Time

Good-by, Sir, excuse me, I haven't time.
I'll come back, I can't wait, I haven't time.
I must end this letter — I haven't time.
I'd love to help you, but I haven't time
I can't accept, having no time.
I can't think, I can't read, I'm swamped, I haven't time
I'd like to pray, but I haven't time.

Michel Quoist

The Paradoxes of Affluence

We had always expected one of the beneficent results of economic affluence to be a tranquil and harmonious manner of life, a life in Arcadia. What has happened is the exact opposite. The pace is quickening, and our lives in fact are becoming steadily more hectic. It used to be assumed that, as the general welfare increased, people would become successively less interested in further rises in income. And yet in practice a still higher economic growth rate has become the overriding goal of economic policy in the rich countries, and the goal also of our private efforts and attitudes. At the same time, much of our expenditure is no longer subject to any very careful consideration, as is clear from the successes noted by Madison Avenue. A growing proportion of the labor force is employed in the service sector, but in spite of this, our resources are in fact less well "serviced" or maintained than ever. It is becoming increasingly difficult, for instance, for elderly people to obtain the special kind of service — care and attention — that they very much need. Our so-called service economy practices in reality a throw-away system at all levels, including the human level. We have long expressed hopes that the elimination of material cares would clear the way for a broad cultural advancement. In practice, not even those endowed with the necessary intellectual and emotional capacity have shown any propensity for immersing themselves in the cultivation of their minds and spirit. The tendency is rather the reverse.

These are but a few examples of the surprising phenomena occurring in the rich countries. They seem paradoxical, as they fail to fit into the picture of affluence which we have painted. The cause of these and similar modern anomalies lies in a circumstance that has been entirely ignored, namely the increasing scarcity of time. The limited availability of time and the increasing claims made on it mean that our affluence is only *partial* and not total as we seem to believe. Our affluence takes only the form of access to *goods*. The idea of "total affluence" is a logical fallacy.

Time as a Scarce Commodity

In the natural sciences, the concept of time offers its particular mysteries. The ultimate implications of time, however, are a problem upon which we need not linger. It will be sufficient for our purposes to accept that there exists what we experience as a time dimension — a moving belt of time units which makes resources of time available to the individual as it passes. Time, unlike other economic resources, cannot be accumulated. We cannot build up a stock of time as we build up a stock of capital. As it passes, however, time puts into people's hands something that they can use. In economic terms, there exists a certain "supply of time."

But there is also a certain "demand for time." Time can be used by individuals in work, with a view to acquiring various goods. Time can also be used in consumption, i.e., the process in which goods are combined with time, in attempts to achieve the ultimate utility in the economic process — material and spiritual well-being. It is important to realize that consumption requires time just as does production.

Such pleasures as a cup of coffee or a good stage play are not in fact pleasurable, unless we can devote time to enjoying them.

The scarcity of a commodity is determined by the supply in relation to the demand. Such a scarcity is normally reflected in the price. The demand for gold is high in relation to the supply, and gold, therefore, attracts a considerable price. The supply of sea water, on the other hand, is extremely great in relation to the demand, and sea water accordingly attracts no price at all. As regards the commodity in which we are interested, namely time, we have already noted that there is a certain supply and a certain demand. We can now add that the demand by individuals is usually sufficiently high in relation to the supply to make time a "scarce commodity" in the economic sense. But if time is an economic utility in short supply, then it must be subject to the economic laws that prevail in the economist's universe. It must be distributed over its different sectors of use — different activities — in accordance with the general principles of economics.

When spending money, one presumably tries to balance one's expenditures in such a way as to obtain the best possible yield. This means that one will probably refrain from spending all one's assets on a single commodity. One will instead distribute one's expenditure over a variety of different goods and services. The optimum situation will have been reached when it is impossible to increase satisfaction by reducing expenditure in one field and making a corresponding increase in another. A more technical description of this condition of equilibrium would be to say that the marginal utility of one dollar must be the same in all different sectors of expenditure.

In the same way, one tries to economize with one's time resources. They must be so distributed as to give an equal yield in all sectors of use. Otherwise, it would pay to transfer time from an activity with a low yield to one with a high yield and to continue to do this until equilibrium had been reached.

Some of my readers may object, perhaps, that this is a somewhat gross description of how people function. A moment's reflection, however, will reveal that if the reader should for this reason put down the book, such a reaction is in itself evidence that people actually try to allocate their time in order to achieve a maximum yield. Such a reader has the impression that it would be a waste of time to spend a couple of hours reading this essay and, therefore, decides to devote his time to some other, and he hopes better, pursuit.

The Increasing Scarcity of Time

The yield on time spent working increases as the result of economic growth. Productivity per hour rises. This means that the time allocation which has represented equilibrium at our previous level of income is disrupted. The yield on time devoted to other activities must also be raised. We are aware that time in production becomes increasingly scarce with economic growth. What we will now claim in addition to this is that changes in the use of time will occur, so that the yield on time in all other activities is brought into parity with the yield on working time. In other words, economic growth entails a general increase in the scarcity of time.

The necessary increase in the yield of time in the nonwork activities can take place in many different ways. To some extent we try to achieve a change in attitudes of a kind that Walter Kerr points out in his book *The Decline of Pleasure:* "We are all of us compelled to read for profit, party for contacts, lunch for contracts, bowl for unity, drive for mileage, gamble for charity, go out for the evening for the greater glory of the municipality, and stay home for the weekend to rebuild the house."

A more basic and radical method of raising the yield on time used in consumption is to increase the amount of consumer goods to be enjoyed per time unit. Just as working time becomes more productive when combined with more capital, so consumption time can give a higher yield when combined with more consumer goods. When this happens, the proportion between consumption goods and the time for consumption changes, so that the price of such time rises to the level of the price of time in production. Admittedly, no prices are openly quoted for time in consumption, but the individual will consciously or unconsciously apply in his actions and words what we can call a "shadow price" to consumption time. This price will go up in step with the productivity of work time.

A critical reader may object that the increasing volume of consumer goods will not necessarily raise the demand for consumption time, but rather the reverse. Many consumer goods, it is claimed, save time. If a household increases its consumption by buying a washing machine, for instance, then the machine will not claim any additional time. It is true that there are many goods of this type. This must be borne in mind when deciding what to classify as "consumer goods." We normally mean all the goods bought by households. In the present study, however, we are considering a more limited category of goods. By "consumption goods," which is the term we shall be using from now on, we mean the definite end products that are combined with time in an attempt to create material or spiritual well-being. Washing machines belong to that category of goods which increases productivity in working life — in this case the work performed within households. We should not make any sharp distinction between activities within households and in production. Many of the former are by nature identical with work in production. Whether productivity rises at places of work within production proper, or in the household, it will have the same effects. The scarcity of time in working life as a whole has increased, and the yield from time in consumption must be increased to create an equilibrium between the yield on time in different sectors. This takes place by an increase in the volume of consumption goods per time unit in consumption.

As already observed, scarce commodities are distributed over different sectors of use in accordance with the principles of economics. Changes in the scarcity of different resources lead to changes in the distribution of resources. These changes, too, follow economic laws. The consequences of an increasing scarcity of time can, therefore, be studied with simple tools borrowed from the practice of economic analysis.

A Basic Problem in Social Science

The analysis of the distribution of time, of changes in this distribution arising from economic growth, and of the implications of economic development under an increasing scarcity of time is not something of purely economic interest. It is rather a problem of more general interest, a joint problem for all the social sciences. The distribution of time and changes in this distribution are bound to affect our entire attitude to social problems, our entire philosophical outlook. An increasing scarcity of time is bound to color our basic attitude to time and pace. David M. Potter in *People of Plenty* has made the incipient superfluity of goods the starting point of speculations as to changes in the national character; the same can be done with the emerging scarcity of time.

A brief study of the literature shows that workers in the different social sciences have in fact shown some interest in the problems of time. It is equally clear, however, that no concerted attack on the problem is being made. In social anthropology, a number of attempts have been made to describe attitudes to time in different cultures. However, many standard works on the subject fail to consider attitudes to time. At all events, hardly any generalizations have been made concerning the factors which determine disparities in time attitudes among different cultures.

The sociologists, for their part, have made great efforts to perform large-scale time-budget studies. They have tried to plot how different individuals or groups divide up their time between various activities. Particularly detailed studies have been made of the use of time spent outside the place of work, time which is devoted to a variety of different activities. However, the theories formed parallel to these studies have been of an ad hoc nature. Attempts at any systematic explanation of time allocation and changes in it are lacking. Because they have ignored the importance of a time scarcity in the economic sense for the time phenomena studied, the anthropologists and sociologists have never really been able to use their own results. It is possible that an analysis of time allocation could yield a dynamic theory for use in sociological predictions. It could be a useful tool in the study of the future, a field of research which affects an increasing amount of attention.

A theory on changes in the scarcity of time could perhaps also be of use in medical research on stress. Similar openings may exist in psychology, perhaps even more in psychiatry. The present writer has found an interest in questions of the type discussed in at least one psychiatric paper. The following quotation from Professor of Psychology John Cohen speaks for itself: "The reaction of animals under conditions of temporal constraint may help to understand human disorders in the tightly time-bound cultures of our day."

It is hardly surprising that sociologists, for instance, have not come to regard the use of time as a problem of economizing with an increasingly scarce commodity. Such an approach, however, should be natural for that science which is devoted to the principles of allocating scarce resources, namely economics. Even so, a reasonable analysis of time is lacking in the economic literature. Economists typically regard consumption as an instantaneous act without temporal consequences. They regard time in working life as a scarce resource, parallel to which there exists some sort of undefined "free time." As incomes rise, one would have increasing consumption, without any consequences to the time situation of the individual, other than a reduction in work time. This would give an increasing amount of "free time." The supply would be increasing on all fronts.

By such a view, the distribution of time can never be made the subject of analysis with the tools of economic theory. It is indeed interesting to see how poorly incorporated free time is in economic theory. To give an example, one ambitious statistical study (by Gordon C. Winston) on the relationship between working time and level of income in different countries makes a distinction between the time used "either on the earning of income (work), or on a host of alternative noneconomic activities (leisure)." To speak of nonworking time as a noneconomic use of time in symptomatic. The very term free time suggests a failure to realize that consumption time is a scarce commodity.

That consumption is regarded as some sort of instantaneous act emerges most clearly from the fact that, when economists try to state the connection between the "utility" of a certain commodity and the amount of that commodity available, they never take into account the time an individual has at his disposal to consume the commodity in question. In economic theory, the pleasure an individual can be expected to derive from a couple of theatre tickets is not taken to be dependent in any way on the time he can devote to playgoing. At most, economic writers take into account the time needed for consumption by pointing out that the utility of a product depends on the length of the time period within which it is to be enjoyed. "Different levels of satisfaction are derived from consuming ten portions of ice cream within one hour and within one month." This point made by J. M. Henderson and R. E. Quandt in their textbook is, however, by no means sufficient. It is not enough to know whether portions of ice cream are to be consumed within a month or within a year. It is far more important to know how much time within a given period can be specifically devoted to enjoying the commodity whose contribution to our material well-being we are studying. If one has no time during a whole week to drink coffee, then obviously even whole sacks full of coffee will give no yield that week. Similarly, a tennis player has no use for a new racket each year, if he never has the time to play. The utility of theatre tickets cannot be established without knowing whether or not the ticket holder has time to use them. What makes the difference is not so much the period of time during which a given quantity of the commodity is available, but rather the time that is available during this period to consume the commodity in question.

Now that we have made these critical observations, we can note with satisfaction that a handful of economists has in recent years adopted a new position. Attention is beginning to be paid to the possibility that economic growth causes an increasing scarcity of time. The first, apparently, in this exclusive group was Roy Harrod, who published a short paper on this theme at the end of the fifties. However, no attention was paid to it by the profession and not even by its author either, since he has never followed up the ideas which he had presented. Harrod's thesis was that we may in time be faced with a consumption maximum, owing to an increasing scarcity of time, which is the result primarily of all the servicing and maintenance work required by consumption goods. It is Harrod's idea, puzzling at first sight, which originally triggered the thinking of the present study.

Another economist who has allowed for the fact that consumption takes time and as a result reached interesting results is Jacob Mincer. Only one economist, however, has attempted to formulate a general theory of time allocation. This is Gary Becker, whose work is presented in a paper published in 1965. The basic approach in this book and in Becker's paper are the same. Even though work on this book had reached a relatively late stage before Becker's paper became available, it has naturally been extremely valuable to be able to utilize Becker's line of thinking.

Why This Neglect of Time Analysis?

The absence of any theory of time allocation in the behavioral sciences must be blamed on economists who, being professionally concerned with the allocation of scarce resources, should certainly have come to regard time in this way. Instead, by ignoring the fact that consumption requires time, they have conveyed the opposite impression — that the use of time off the job is a noneconomic phenomenon and that economic growth results in a decreasing scarcity of time. How can we explain this neglect on the part of the economists? In the absence of any entirely convincing or sufficient explanation, we can only suggest various possibilities. To begin with, there could be a historical reason. When the first economists defined their sphere of interest, the scarcity of time was hardly noticeable. The overriding problem was the scarcity of goods as a result of low productivity. It was, therefore, reasonable to speak of free time in the true economic sense, i.e., time without a price. Consumption goods were lacking, and marginal time was perhaps spent in enforced passivity. Fettered by an analytic tradition, economists have failed to see time as a scarce resource, even though the situation has radically changed.

It is also possible that the actual term economic growth is misleading. When we speak of economic growth, it is easy to think of growing economic opportunities in general. We imagine total, rather than partial, affluence. Obviously, such an erroneous picture will emerge more easily if we are unaware that consumption takes time, and we stare blindly at various statistical theories reporting that we not only have more and more goods but also more and more free time. Some people may also entertain a vague idea that there has been some sort of technological advance in consumption, so that the demand for time has remained constant. But insofar as any technological advances have been made on the consumer side, they must relate to the individual's work in the household. The effects of such technological advances, however, are the same as in production proper. It is difficult to conceive of any technological advance being noted in the actual process of consumption. Productivity can be purchased only by an increase in the quantity of goods consumed per time unit, which means an increased scarcity of time.

Another possibility is that people have disregarded the claims made on consumption time because of certain basic conceptions of how our growing material affluence might be used. The optimistic view has prevailed that people would gradually be freed from toil and starvation, in order to devote themselves to cultivation of the mind and spirit in accordance with the ideals of classical antiquity. On these terms, what we now mean by consumption would take very little time. The economic target would be met as soon as we had reached a material level permitting uninterrupted philosophical exercises. Neither time nor material goods would be scarce commodities, the economic problem would vanish with the attainment of complete satisfaction in the embrace of the fine arts and beautiful thoughts. This picture has been belied by events. As economic development has continued, attractive alternative ways of using time have emerged. Mediation and speculation have been driven off the market. Whatever the cause, time has thus become de facto an increasingly scarce resource, without the economists having noticed this development.

The So-called "Leisure Problem"

Many will surely find it peculiar that economic development should result in an increasing scarcity of time. One imagines that the situation should be the reverse. Intellectuals of the rich countries fail to analyze the increasing scarcity of time, but instead devote a great deal of attention to the so-called leisure problem.

What in fact is this much publicized but undefined leisure problem? Does it mean that people, because of the shorter working week, have got so much time on their hands that they do not know what to do with it? This would mean that time had become less and less scarce, and that there is something ludicrously amiss with the whole basic idea of this book. Instead of an increasing scarcity of time we should have a surplus.

But even if the leisure problem can not be taken to mean that people do nothing, it may nonetheless exist. However, it then consists of some people busying themselves with nothingness — a problem which is not in conflict with the argument made in this essay.

The leisure problem of the economic type, however, probably exists only in the imagination of those who are unaware that consumption takes time. If we take the position, like most economists, that consumption is instantaneous and that free time is some entirely isolated utility, then it is possible to draw peculiar conclusions. We can imagine, in this case, that we now have so much free time that we do not know what to do with it, and that certain parts of this time are reduced to what we have called economic free time. It may be that some people are in such a situation. They have a job, and they make a certain amount of money. This is used to purchase consumption goods, the enjoyment of which takes a certain time. When they have consumed these goods, people then spend the rest of their time in complete passivity. Such a mode of life, however, would seem uncommon. If people have more time left over for consumption than they think they need, most of them surely take some form of extra work. This gives them more money which they can use in consumption and thus absorb consumption time. Insofar as they do not do this, it must mean that they have reached a maximum for their consumption. The existence of any such ceiling, however, is energetically denied, at least by economists and by psychologists interested in economics.

There is no guarantee, after all, that people will devote their time off the job to entirely laudable ends. On the contrary, it is probable that many people choose to expend their increasing resources in a manner injurious to themselves and their environment. Such individuals, however, are not idle. They can be extremely busy in all sorts of mischief. This is a very real problem, but it is obviously no leisure problem, in the sense that people do not know what to do with, all their time. It is a social problem. The fact that people use their money in a dangerous way does not eliminate the need for economic theory. In the same way, the fact that people sometimes use their time in dangerous ways does not mean that we do not need a theory of time allocation.

It is obviously possible also to worry over the fact that so many people occupy themselves, if not with mischief, at least with such vacuous practices as reading comics and drinking Coca-Cola. This too is something that can lead people to talk of a leisure problem. For moral, ethical, cultural, or other reasons, they cannot accept the way in which others choose to use their time. Here again; we have a problem relating not to economic free time, but to the quality of our civilization. Superficial people in the rich countries are often in a greater hurry than anyone else. They are enormously busy, even if it is sometimes difficult to see with what.

There is yet another interpretation of what leisure problem might mean. Many have expressed the fear that, as there is less demand on the individual to contribute work, we shall loose something essential to personal human value. This is an important risk, and one that we must take into consideration when assessing what higher productivity is really giving us. Here again, it is not a question of our nonworking time becoming economic free time. The underlying idea is simply that the compulsion to work confers a greater value on the individual than the freedom to consume. The problem is a psychological one.

It seems reasonable to draw the conclusion that leisure problems of a social, cultural, and psychological nature exist. But the average earner in the rich country lives nonetheless under the pressure of time. He is a member of the harried leisure class.

A Framework for Discussion

In the economic land of dreams that many see as the end result of a long process of growth, the inherent thrift of nature would be overcome. It is only by a sort of optical illusion that one can imagine this meanness on nature's part being eliminated in a material Utopia. In an economic heaven, the problem of time will be particularly pressing. We will find there an infinite volume of consumption goods, which pleasure-hungry angels will feverishly try to exploit during the limited time at their disposal per day. That one may in this heaven enjoy eternal life as a consumer fails to alter the situation. This can increase the total satisfaction derived over the course of centuries. What we are interested in, however, is the yield per time unit. To maximize this, time must be carefully stewarded by the servants of epicureanism.

To map the changes that economic growth will cause in the way we employ our time, it is convenient to classify time into different categories. Such a division of time into different areas of use could obviously be very detailed. Any minute classification, however, would be impractical. We will distinguish below between five different categories of time, each of which has been considered unequal from a philosophical point of view. Each of them is affected in different ways by economic growth.

The first category of time is working time or, more specifically, time spent working in specialized production. Such working time is of basic importance to the allocation of time. Like other activities, it claims time that could otherwise be spent in other ways. However, by its effect on the income level of the individual, it also influences the amount of time in demand for other activities. Work time is thus of twofold importance. It affects both the supply and the demand for time on other activities. As the level of productivity in working life changes, work time and the level of income send out impulses for the changes that can be made in allocation of time.

The second category we can call time for personal work. Personal work consists essentially of the production of what we customarily term services. The boundaries between the production of services and

goods are elusive, but it is usually drawn. In the industrialized countries, the production of goods is almost entirely specialized. A large
proportion of services is also the result of specialized production. We
are left, even so, with a considerable number of services to produce
on our own. Even the members of Thorstein Veblen's golden leisure
class, who by no means lacked the economic resources to buy services, were surely reduced to providing many services for themselves.
The scope of personal work of the average earner in a highly industrialized country is surely considerably greater. Personal work can be
subdivided into the maintenance of goods and of one's body (sleep,
personal hygiene, etc.). We shall be interesting ourselves not only in
the total time each individual devotes to personal work, but also to
the average maintenance time devoted to consumption goods, i.e., the
maintenance time per consumption good.

A third category is consumption time, i.e., the time, the existence
of which we must be aware of, in order to see the use of time as an
economic problem involving the allocation of limited resources. Just
as with time for personal work, there is a correlation between increases in productivity and the demand for consumption time. Again
in this case, we shall investigate the changes in consumption time per
product.

The fourth component comprises time devoted to the cultivation of
mind and spirit, i.e., the various exercises to which the optimistic
believers in progress had thought we would devote our affluence. The
difference between consumption time and what, for the sake of brev-
ity, we may call culture time is that consumption goods play a central
role for consumption time, but only an incidental role for culture
time. For this reason, these two time components are affected in
different ways by any productivity increase in working life. The distinction between these two components is of even greater importance
in that they have been so differently judged in discussions relating to
the aims of the economic process.

Finally, we have a time component that is less specific in its nature. It is conceivable that people in the poor countries are subjected
to free time in the strict sense of the word, i.e., time that is not
utilized. Incomes are so low that people fail to obtain an economic

level permitting anything except what we can call passivity during
certain periods of the day. Such time can also occur in the rich countries during economic depressions. But even when economic circumstances are such that individuals are in a position to choose freely
how they will distribute their time between work and other activities,
there can still be what we can call "slacks" in the use of time. This
finds expression in the pace at which time is used. If the scarcity of
time is not particularly marked, people may find it reasonable to
enjoy a relaxed life. We will call this fifth and last category of time
idleness.

In Chapter II we shall discuss changes in idleness and in the pace
of existence. Chapter III contains a discussion of changes in work
time. Chapter IV to VI discuss time for personal work. The last of
these three chapters is devoted to changes in time for decision-
making. Consumption time is treated in Chapter VII and in Chapter
VIII we will investigate changes in culture time. A more special
problem is considered in Chapter IX, where we shall discuss the relationship between saving and time allocation. In Chapters II to XI
we assume that per capita incomes are steadily increasing. In the
three closing chapters (X to XII) we shall investigate how far the
results of our time allocation analysis have affected the credibility of
this assumption of continued economic growth. A list of notes and
references is given at the end of the book. Certain arguments basic
to the discussion are presented mathematically in an appendix.

CHAPTER II

The Disappearance of Idleness

We may note at this point the differences
in the value and calibration of time among
peoples at different levels of culture.

John Cohen

An Increasing Degree of Utilization

The scope of idleness depends on the level of income. If incomes are low, there can be long periods of enforced idleness or passivity. Individuals will then have at their disposal economic free time in the true sense. They are waiting for Godot. At a higher level of income we find voluntarily chosen idleness, which is reflected in people taking life easy and finding this enjoyable. The pace of life is not rapid. But as incomes continue to rise, the demands for yield on the use of time increase. As a result, fewer and fewer "slacks" will be tolerated. The degree to which time is actively utilized will increase. The pace of life will quicken.

The economic reasons for these changes are easy to discern. Time spent in idleness, unlike actively utilized time, cannot give a higher yield by being combined with more consumption goods. By definition, idleness is time spent without other consumption goods. In some way, however, the yield must also be raised on this type of time. As shown in an "equation of hecticness" in the mathematical appendix, one will, in order to achieve this, reduce such time and transfer bits of it to active use. In this way, the faster the pace becomes, the greater will be the yield on time still spent in idleness. New positions of equilibrium in the allocation of time can be reached in this way as incomes rise.

It is not difficult, in practice, to find radical discrepancies in the conception of time among different cultures. There also seems to be a clear connection between level of income and the role played by time and its exploitations. If this is the case, then one should draw entirely different conclusions from those customarily drawn in the anthropological literature, which describes such discrepancies as due to differences in cosmological concepts and technological development. To develop this idea further, we can distinguish among three different types of culture, namely cultures with a time surplus, cultures with a time affluence, and cultures suffering from a time famine.

Cultures with a Time Surplus

Cultures with a superfluity of time are to be found in the poorest countries. Productivity is so low that a certain proportion of time yields nothing whatsoever. Such cultures have no great need of precision in reckoning and measuring time. We find there a *mañana* attitude, with no detailed planning for either today or tomorrow. In fact, what we in the rich countries mean by time is a concept difficult to translate into the languages of these cultures. In the rich countries, a time surplus can also exist if the demand for labor is low, as during a depression. Handicapped individuals who are excluded from the labor market and the growth process, and who consequently have low incomes, also may experience a time surplus.

Obviously, it is difficult in practice to determine whether or not a given amount of time per day is economic free time. The boundary is difficult to draw. Even so, for analytic purposes we may consider as a difference in kind what may be a difference in degree. Time which gives no yield need not be spent, literally, in complete passivity. Various kinds of hidden unproductive time can occur. The literature on the underdeveloped countries, for instance, speaks fairly frequently of "disguised underemployment." Such underemployment exists if a reduction in working time does not reduce production. It has been claimed that this is one characteristic of agriculture in the underdeveloped countries. This view has not gone uncriticized, but most of the criticism directed against the notion of hidden unemployment in the agriculture of these countries is related to the cavalier conclusions drawn from it with respect to economic policy.

Unemployment or underemployment in the often fast growing cities in these countries is more overt. The shantytowns are jam-packed with people who spend at least part of their day in enforced idleness. This may take the form of fruitless attempts on the part of some people to find gainful employment while others resign themselves to begging. A stuporous passivity is one way of passing such enforced economic free time. One way of promoting economic free time to a higher status is to devote it to improving one's chances of a better life in the next world. One can designate a large number of days as holy days, or "holidays," in the original sense of the word. It has been pointed out that the number of such holidays is greater in the poor countries than in the rich, and that on the road to riches a country gradually eliminates more and more holidays, reducing the amount of economic free time. "It should be remembered too that throughout antiquity and the Middle Ages the normal number of holidays during the year was about 115," writes Ida Craven. As the need for consumption time in the rich countries became marked, the holy days became holidays or vacations — an entirely different category of time from our point of view.

An interesting picture of how the attitude to time in poor cultures differs from what we are used to is given by the anthropological literature. We can only regret that the mapping of different cultures' conceptions of time is not, to judge from the literature, taken as a very important task of anthropological research.

One rewarding source is a report compiled by a team under the leadership of Margaret Mead. This team performed a number of comparative anthropological studies, also including attitudes to time. We can see what enormous differences exist in these respects between, on the one hand, Burma and the Spanish-American subculture in the United States, and on the other hand, the rich countries. Differences between the two poor cultures with respect to time concepts appear to be small. The degree of utilization of time is in both cases low. We are told, for instance, how the Burmese have various simple methods of measuring time, how Spanish-Americans abstain from regulating their existence by clocks, and how they plan their future time only vaguely, or not at all.

Edward T. Hall has made the same sort of observations in his book *The Silent Language:* "[With] the people of the Middle East . . . it is pointless to make an appointment too far in advance, because the informal structure of their time system places everything beyond a week into a single category of 'future', in which plans tend to 'slip off their minds'."

As regards the lack of any time concept corresponding to that in the rich countries, no one could be more explicit than Evans-Pritchard in his study of the Nuer:*

Though I have spoken of time and units of time the Nuer have no expression equivalent to time in our language, and they cannot, therefore, as we can, speak of time as though it were something actual, which passes, can be wasted, can be saved, and so forth. I do not think that they ever experienced the same feeling of fighting against time or of having to co-ordinate activities with an abstract passage of time, because their points of reference are mainly the activities themselves, which are generally of a leisurely character. Events follow a logical order, but they are not controlled by an abstract system, there being no autonomous points of reference to which activities have to conform with precision. Nuer are fortunate.

The concept of time among the Tiv in Nigeria has been studied by Paul Bohannan. He emphasizes also that time is a word very difficult to translate, that time is indicated on the basis of natural phenomena, or social events, instead of within a chronological system, and that "thus although Tiv indicate time by direct association of two events, and though they count recurrent natural units such as days, markets, moons, and dry seasons, they do not measure time."

These and similar observations from many different cultures can be given a uniform explanation within the framework of a time allocation theory. The level of income is extremely low, and time is, therefore, not scarce.

* A pastoral people living in the Anglo-Egyptian Sudan.

Time Affluence Cultures

Cultures with an adequate supply of time occupy a middle position. A process of economic growth has started, and the level of incomes has been doubled or tripled. The pace of life has, therefore, increased, but it has not yet become hectic. The long stretches of economic free time have all disappeared. Certain slacks in the use of time remain, however. Methods of measuring time have been improved, but the clock is not yet a tyrant. There is also a certain, but not yet detailed, planning of the use of time. Poor Richard's statement in his almanack that "Those who use their time the worst, will be the first to complain about its shortness" begins to apply.

Let us consider what author Vilhelm Moberg has to say of his childhood in the early part of this century, i.e., in a Sweden where the general level of income had not yet attained any great heights:

No one in my childhood was in a hurry. They did quite a lot of work, usually very hard work, but they never gave evidence of any haste. When I left this environment in due course and returned to the home of my parents on a visit, my father observed my nervous unrest and asked: — Why in such a hurry, boy? You'll get to your grave in time, like everyone else.

Japan, as yet, is in this intermediate category from the point of view of income. There seems to exist in Japan an attitude to time and its use that is what we might expect from the theory here proposed. Robert J. Smith describes the Japanese attitude to time as follows:

One feature of Japanese life which makes adjustment in the later years rather easier than it is in some societies is the concept of time and its scheduling in Japanese society. The Japanese are not tyrannized by the clock, nor is there an emphasis on scheduling of activities. Both work and leisure-time activities tend to follow an unpredictable pattern. Japanese white-collar workers, for example, think little of working extra hours or even through the night without extra compensation if requested to do so. Meals are not necessarily eaten on a schedule, and missing a meal is no great tragedy. The approach to appointments is notoriously casual, and it is worth pointing out that a guest may arrive before or after a casually agreed-upon hour. Pre-arrangement of appointments is not considered essential, for it is expected that everyone's schedule is sufficiently flexible to permit him to adjust his activities to any emergency which may arise. Not even the changes wrought by the last hundred years of industrialization have completely altered this picture.

We can also quote the Mead report again. This offers some interesting information on attitudes to time in Greece, another country which is neither rich nor poor.

Greeks 'pass' the time; they do not save or accumulate or use it. And they are intent on passing the time, not on budgeting it. Although city people say that this picture is changing, that they are now made aware of the need to use time, the attitude is still widely prevalent, even in the area of private life among the urban groups.

The clock is not master of the Greek: it does not tell him to get up, to go to the field. In most villages, in spite of recent changes, the peasants still get up at sunrise or dawn to go to the fields, and return at sundown. The day is made for work. At night women visit and gossip; men join them or go to the coffee house; there is storytelling, and ardent political discussion; and as for any work done after dark, 'the day takes a look at it and laughs.' Wherever there is no law to the contrary, a man opens his store in due course, not by the clock; however, in the cities he now functions under clocked time, because he comes under government and union regulations. . . . It is distasteful to Greeks to organize their activities according to external limits; they are therefore either early or late, if a time is set at all. At church the people are not impatient while waiting for Mass to begin; and the church fills only gradually. They know when to go to church; yet when a foreign visitor inquires as to the time of a certain Mass, the subject creates a discussion; and eventually the answer will be something like: 'Between 2 and 3.' And when Greeks who follow their traditional ways invite, they say, not 'Come at 7 o'clock,' but 'Come and see us.' To arrive to dinner on time is an insult, as if you came just for the food. You come to visit, and the dinner eventually appears. Among urbanized Greeks, this custom now seems burdensome, and there are many cartoons on the subject.

The dinner is not planned to appear at a predetermined time; and the housewife does not cook by the clock. She tells by the smell or the consistency, or the colour, or the resistance against the stirring spoon; or the passing of time is gauged by the intervening activities . . .

Greek men and women work expeditiously, as a rule, but do this best at their own rhythm; any need to hurry is external and interfering; it introduces fuss and disturbance. Efficiency can usually be found when it is not a conscious end.

To introduce an awareness of time into a meal is particularly abhorrent to Greeks, though this has to be done where factories set time limits. Dinner is served when it is ready, and without regard to efficient consumption. The fish is not fileted, and nuts are not shelled, the fruit is not sliced. The eater will spend a long time removing infinitesimal bits of flesh from the head of a small fish. All this is part of the process of eating, which is more than the naked act of consumption . . . Greeks in the city, in some circles, find the need of hurry entering their lives. They are not at home with it. For the Greek traditionally, to work against time, to hurry, is to forfeit freedom. His term for hurry means, originally, to coerce oneself . . .

In spite of the prevalence of timepieces, the church bell and the school bell, and even a cannon blast, continue to have active functions in calling adults or children to pre-arranged gatherings or communal village work. Even in the cities, people are called 'Englishmen' when they turn up on the dot at meetings or appointments. People often arrive an hour late to an appointment to find that the other person is also just arriving, or, if they find him gone, they usually accept the fact with neither apology nor frustration.

In our attempt to understand the influence of income increases on the scarcity of time, and thus on the mode of life, it is particularly interesting to see the changes in attitude to time occurring in the cities, changes to which the report gives special emphasis. The level of income is probably higher in the cities, so that the growing scarcity of time is first felt there.

Time Famine Cultures

Walter Kerr has expressed his surprise at the increasing tempo of life as follows: "Isn't it odd that a century which should, by all rights, be the most leisurely in all history is also known to be, and condemned for being, the fastest?"

What has happened is that in the rich countries all slacks in the use of time have been eliminated, so far as is humanly possible. The attitude to time is dictated entirely by the commodity's extreme scarcity. The day of the sluggard is over. "Personal administration" has become important. We may not be terribly good at it, but we are aware that it is a desirable skill. The pocket calendar becomes our most important book. Its loss causes the owner himself to feel lost. Punctuality has become a virtue that we demand of those around us. Waiting is a squandering of time that angers people in rich countries. Only personal mismanagement, or the inconsiderate behavior of others, will create brief — and highly irritating — periods of involuntary idleness. People are dominated by their awareness of the clock. They are haunted by their knowledge that the shining moments are passing without things having been done. The clock in Times Square shows what second it is to those hurrying by. As George Woodcock has pointed out, we live under the tyranny of the clock. This tyranny has developed, step by step, with our successful revolution against the dictatorship of material poverty.

This description of a culture suffering from a time famine may seem exaggerated, and so it may be, if it is only seen as a description of present conditions. It will become increasingly accurate as the level of income continues to rise. Even now, it fits many environments. An insight into time attitudes and the mode of life to which they give rise in the rich countries can be obtained from a book like *Crestwood Heights,* the result of five years' intensive study of life in a wealthy Canadian suburb. The three authors J. R. Seeley, R. A. Sim, and E. W. Loosley are sociologists and psychologists. They devote one chapter to describing attitudes to time. The picture that emerges gives us a vivid idea of life in a time famine culture.

In Crestwood Heights time seems almost the paramount dimension of existence . . . An urban population with its ramifying interdependencies is almost compelled to adopt synchronized schedules . . . His wife has her own activities outside the home which are carefully scheduled . . . The chlidren have their school — which demands punctuality — scheduled appointments with dentists and dancing teacher, and numerous social activities. Home life is indeed often hectic . . . But the very nature of secondary group life beyond the primary, family circle can hardly permit too much of this simplicity, and the resultant schedules are so demanding that the parents feel themselves constantly impelled to inculcate the virtues of punctuality and regularity in themselves and the child, at meal hour, departures for picnics, and such occasions. . . . The activity promoted by the institution [church, bookclub, and the like] is regulated by the clock, and the schedule of one institution, unless it is definitely raiding the time and clientele of the other, must be fitted to the schedule of others within an inevitably tight competition for time . . . The phenomenon which the Crestwooder calls 'pressure' is caused by this concentration of demands into limited units of time. A mother will say 'I get so I can't cope with everything.' No one is more admired than the person who is 'never ruffled,' who keeps the flow steady . . . The ubiquitous desk calendar and appointment book facilitate this flow.

A lot of similar material could be quoted. The reader may be interested — and surprised — to learn that Stockholmers are so interested in keeping an eye on the time that they made in 1966 no fewer than eighteen million telephone calls to "Miss Time," or about fifteen calls per capita. The number of calls per apparatus 1955–1965 increased from eighteen to twenty-two, although the number of apparatus during this period increased more than did the number of individuals. This circumstance and corresponding figures from other countries and towns suggest that the majority of readers has personal experience of life by a strict timetable.

In Praise of Idleness

The anthropological and sociological material that we have quoted at least does not gainsay the thesis that a dwindling scarcity of goods entails an increasing scarcity of time, and that these relative changes leave deep marks in a society's mode of life. What are we to think of this increasing tempo? Our ultimate judgment, if such a thing is possible, must be deferred until we have had occasion to study in more detail the effects of economic development or the uses of time in other respects than this increasing tempo of life. Even at this stage, however, there is reason to make certain limited comments on what the increase in tempo may mean.

We can note, to begin with, that it entails certain risks of an actual decline in the efficiency with which time is used. One can obtain blocking phenomena of the same type as when traffic routes are overloaded. Too many vehicles crowd together and prevent each other's movements. Time is a route into which we can try to press so much that traffic is jammed even to chaos.

An alternative way of seeing these difficulties is as disruptions resulting from overemployment. Full employment of our time capacity is perhaps a good thing, but there may also occur a form of overfull employment which is ineffective — just as on the labor market overfull employment can lead to a less productive use of resources. At the personal level, this means a risk of stress. A fully packed schedule can lead to our jumping from one task to another and actually performing less than would otherwise be possible. In the worst case — and this is no uncommon thing in a time famine — people die an early death from overstrain and insufficient time instead of, as previously, from a shortage of goods. Deaths are now caused by high productivity, not low productivity.

The ability to administrate one's resources of time effectively varies enormously between individuals. It is, therefore, hardly surprising that people in a society suffering from a time famine greatly admire those who are capable of maintaining a high tempo without breaking down. Recall that the ideal in Crestwood Heights was to be "unruffled." There is a parallel here with the labor market. The meaning of overfull employment will depend largely on how the labor market is organized. With a smoothly functioning labor market, it may be possible to reach very high employment levels without disruptions. On a badly functioning labor market, even 95 per cent employment can cause trouble.

But a high tempo entails a sort of risk other than the risk of inefficiency. There is a real danger that our ability to enjoy all our material utilities will decline in step with our efforts to increase the yield of available time by a more hectic tempo. As they become subjected to the pressure of the time famine, many people feel a Rousseauesque longing for the more tranquil past. The pace and manner of life in Greece as Margaret Mead describes it seem attractive to many people, although through living in a harried culture, they are aware how difficult it would be to try to apply such a style of life in their own environment. Some people experience the pressure of time so strongly that they believe those with a superfluity of time — and thus a poverty of goods — to have been, or to be, happier. Evans-Pritchard's statement, already quoted, that "Nuer are fortunate," since they do not suffer any pressure of time, is symptomatic.

This is something on which everyone must form his own opinion. We must be careful, however, not to adopt inconsistent points of view. The tempo of life in poor countries is admittedly humane, but other conditions are not. Freedom from a poverty of time, is not freedom from all poverty. On the contrary, economic free time in the old days was often spent in mental convulsions of misery. The elimination of such economic free time must be taken as an actual target for a growth process and not simply as an adjustment to increased productivity. We must be careful not to conceive a mythical society in which the material riches of "The Hectic Society" are somehow combined with the superfluity of time existing in materially poor cultures. The two are apparently incompatible.

Is there any possibility of steering between Scylla and Charybdis? Probably there is. But this presupposes that people desire to spend their time in a way that does not involve consumption centered upon goods. If the entire economic process were something subsidiary, something that it might be possible to disengage from material activities, then it would be conceivable to achieve our economic targets rapidly, in order to devote ourselves thereafter to matters outside economic analysis. We would then have achieved complete satisfaction of our material wants. We would find ourselves in an intermediate position with fewer goods, but as many as we needed; and plenty of time, but with sufficient economic resources to devote it to noneconomic matters. This, however, is not the road we have taken. Bertrand Russell, in his essay, "In Praise of Idleness," regrets that we have chosen what he believes to be a ridiculous course. He urges us to see economic progress as a means that can release us from the economic process and permit "idleness," i.e., idleness of the sort devoted to cultivation of the mind. Instead, he says, we are allowing higher productivity to lead to a growing number of material objects, all of which make their demands on us. Russell regrets that we are learning to make twice as many pins in a given time and not to make a given quantity of pins in half the time. This, however, is bound to happen if we have a consumption centered upon goods and see before us a possibility of raising the yield on our time resources by intensifying consumption when increased incomes so permit. This is Russell's complaint: "There was formerly a capacity for light-heartedness and play which has been to some extent inhibited by the cult of efficiency. The modern man thinks that everything ought to be done for the sake of something else, and never for its own sake."

CHAPTER III

Work Time

Work is the only occupation yet
invented which mankind has been
able to endure in any but the
smallest possible doses.

C. E. M. Joad

The Double Effect of Work Time

It is obvious that the different ways of using time are mutually interdependent, and that the allocation of time must be decided simultaneously. The productivity changes, whose consequences we are concerned with studying, exercise their effects via work time, and it is, therefore, suitable to study first changes in the length of working hours. These changes will determine not only how much time is available for other activities, but also how high incomes are at the higher levels of productivity. The average consumption time and maintenance time per consumption item — two important relationships — will thus be determined by the length of work time and changes in this arising from increased productivity.

What is Happening to the Length of Working Hours?

In economic theory, attempts have actually been made to indicate how a productivity increase could effect the amount of free time consumers would choose to have. Since free time is defined in these roughly hewn models as nonwork time, the question of how work time would change is considered simultaneously. It has been impossible, however, on deductive grounds, to reach any conclusion regarding the direction of these changes. Work time may increase or decrease. As productivity rises and incomes, with a constant allocation of time, increase, one can afford to obtain more of the various utilities on which value is placed. This should mean that one will also want more free time and will, therefore, reduce working hours. But when the level of productivity rises, the relative prices of different utilities change. Free time becomes relatively more expensive in relation to everything else. This would make it reasonable to cut down on free time. One thus finds two contrary effects: an income effect directed toward shorter working hours, and a substitution effect directed toward longer working hours. It is impossible to state a priori which of these two forces is the stronger. To decide how work time is influenced by productivity increases is, therefore, a purely empirical problem. The majority of people, it seems, takes it for granted that working hours will decline. A more careful study of the matter — which must be reserved for Chapter XI — shows, however, that the actual changes occurring are far from clear.

Standard economic theory sees consumption as an act without any dimension in time, and regards free time as a separate utility among all others. But even if one regards consumption instead as a process in which time and consumption goods are combined, one has unfortunately not come very much further in determining how work time is influenced by an increase in income. Even if one can remark that an increase in the volume of consumption goods will make certain claims on time for the purposes of maintenance and consumption, one can still not determine whether consumers will prefer to substitute goods for time to such an extent that work time will increase. If we cannot attack the central question without making restrictive assumptions, we can still make certain observations of interest.

To begin with, we should be aware that reductions in idleness can mean increases both in work time and consumption time. This is a likely change, above all during the initial period of economic growth.

Secondly, changes can occur in the degree of specialization. A greater or lesser number of tasks can be performed as personal work. There are forces here acting in different directions. First of all, it is probable that the degree of specialization will rise considerably. Working duties will be transferred from the households to firms. But this increase in what we mean by work time need not mean a reduced time for consumption. The sum of time for specialized work and personal work may have fallen. In poor countries which are in the process of economic growth, we can thus find an increase in both work time and consumption time, owing partly to the absorption of economic free time, partly to an increasing degree of specialization. We have what Arthur Lewis has called "economic development with unlimited supplies of labor." At a later stage of development, it is entirely possible that functions will be transferred in the opposite direction. The degree of specialization will decrease when all goods are already produced outside the households, and an increasing consumption makes growing demands for maintenance work. But in spite of a reduction in the time spent in specialized work, consumption time can still fall. Thirdly, in the case of persons with relatively high hourly earnings, it is to be noted that a higher degree of specialization will be to their advantage. This will, in turn, affect the length of their working hours. Their time allocation, moreover, will not be decided simply by the development of their own productivity, but also by how the average level of productivity develops, since their real income is affected by both these factors. This connection is interesting to explore. A special problem in deciding what length of time is to be spent in specialized work is presented by the level of taxation. This question, which manifestly does not apply exclusively to high earners, will be touched upon in Chapter IX.

Fourthly, it makes a great difference whether a wage increase is temporary or permanent. If it is temporary, then it must lead to an increase in work time. A farmer works longer hours during the harvest than otherwise. A fisherman spends more time at sea when the herring comes in. Everyone probably works harder during those years of life when earning capacity is highest. The reason for allocating one's time in this way is that one has the possibility of saving a certain part of one's income. In this way, one can postpone consumption and maintain an even proportion between consumption goods and consumption time over a longer period. One thus evens out the yield on consumption time, which probably leads to an improvement in total welfare. We shall return to this problem in Chapter IX. Until then, we shall assume that all incomes are spent continuously.

To say anything more about how wage increases will influence the length of working hours, we need to make certain assumptions. A very reasonable assumption is that the volume of consumption goods will increase at least as rapidly as consumption time. The reason why we must suppose that consumption time will not increase more rapidly than the number of goods is that goods will be relatively cheaper than time. One will, therefore, find it suitable to make consumption more "goods intensive." Alternatively, we can say that one will tend to increase the number of goods per time unit in consumption, in order to raise the yield on such time to the same level as in production. Changes in the opposite direction would imply a saturation of wants. Similarly, it seems probable — in fact very likely — that the time spent in maintenance work will not rise more quickly than the volume of goods.

This observation that work time will probably not fall so much as to cause consumption time and maintenance time to increase more rapidly than the volume of goods, does not make it possible to say in what direction work time will change when the level of income rises. It can increase or decrease. We can say only that it cannot decrease *below a certain level* in connection with each wage increase. To reach a number of other conclusions, however, it is perfectly sufficient to know how the proportion between income and time for other activities will change as the level of income rises.

A Numerical Example

To see more precisely how work time changes when the level of income rises, we have to make additional — and now less probable — assumptions. In a numerical example, we will assume that the two important ratios — consumption time and maintenance time per consumption item — are constant. There is thus no possibility of substituting goods for time, when goods become relatively cheaper. This is not particularly probable; as we have noted, it represents a limiting case. However, it is a limiting case that is easy to study in a simple numerical example. Such an example is of great interest because it permits us to see clearly what mutual connections exist between wages and changes in time allocation. The limiting case in question is also illuminating in that it emphasizes the difference between, on the one hand, time reallocations among the five main activities and, on the other, changes within these. By making the two ratios constant — numerically, let us say that the consumption time and maintenance time per product are each half-an-hour per day — we assume that all the changes occurring will mean reallocations in time between the main categories. We can then see what the consequences would be, if these ratios could not in reality be changed. The importance of the changes which we shall be describing in a later chapter will emerge more clearly in this way.

In our example, we will also assume, for the sake of simplicity, that we have only three different time components, namely work time, time in personal work, and consumption time. We will set the total time to be allocated at sixteen hours per day. The rest of the time is assumed to be spent in maintenance work of a kind which is not directly affected by the volume of consumption. This type of personal work comprises time mainly spent on what we can call personal maintenance, for instance in the form of sleep.

The time allocation under these assumptions has been calculated in Table 1 for different levels of productivity. Each column indicates the equilibrium allocation of time at a given level of real wages. If the level of productivity is one unit per working hour, then the time allocation at equilibrium will be to work eight hours and earn eight units. These units (goods) will then require four hours' personal work and four hours' consumption time. We will then have utilized all the time available, namely sixteen hours.

If the level of wages is doubled, then work time will drop to 5⅓ hours. In this time we shall earn 10⅔ units. These will require 5⅓ hours in personal work and 5⅓ in consumption time. All sixteen hours will then be used. If the level of wages rises to three units per working hour, we shall be working for four hours, devoting six hours to personal work and a further six hours to consumption. The total volume of goods in this case will be twelve units. We can see from the last column that when the level of wages tends to infinity, then work time will tend to zero, time for personal work to eight hours, and consumption time also to eight hours. The total volume of consumption goods tends to sixteen units. If we add work time to time spent in personal work, we see that the sum is twelve hours at a wage level of one unit per hour, falling towards eight hours as the level of wages proceeds towards infinity.

TABLE 1

The allocation of time at different productivity levels on the assumption that the proportions between volume of goods and time are fixed both in personal work and consumption, being in each case one half-hour per product

| | Level of Productivity Expressed in No. Consumption Goods Earned per Working Hour | | | | | |
	1	2	3	4	8	→ ∞
Work time	8	$5\frac{1}{3}$	4	$3\frac{1}{5}$	$1\frac{7}{9}$	→ 0
Time in personal work	4	$5\frac{1}{3}$	6	$6\frac{2}{5}$	$7\frac{1}{9}$	→ 8
Sum of work time and time in personal work	12	$10\frac{2}{3}$	10	$9\frac{3}{5}$	$8\frac{8}{9}$	→ 8
Consumption time	4	$5\frac{1}{3}$	6	$6\frac{2}{5}$	$7\frac{1}{9}$	→ 8
Total time	16	16	16	16	16	16
No. of consumption goods (units)	8	$10\frac{2}{3}$	12	$12\frac{4}{5}$	$14\frac{2}{9}$	→ 16

When studying these results, we must naturally never forget that they are based on special assumptions. Apart from the fact that the volume of consumption goods will increase as wages go up, we cannot be certain of the *direction* of the different changes. We know, however, that the reduction in working hours in all probability cannot go faster than we have shown it to do in the above table, since in that case, consumption time would increase more quickly than the volume of goods — a possibility which can be excluded. Consequently, it is established that consumption time cannot increase more quickly than in the table. Nor can the time devoted to personal work increase more rapidly than in our example — at least not without a lower degree of specialization. When we abandon our assumption that the proportions between time and volume of goods are fixed in both personal work and consumption, then work time will decrease more slowly than in Table 1. If it is very easy to substitute goods for consumption time, then the latter may actually increase. If time and consumption goods are not necessarily combined in fixed proportions, it will also mean — and this is a very important consequence — that the volume of consumption goods need not travel towards a maximum as it does in our example.

The Work Time of High Income Earners

We have assumed so far that every individual personally handles the entire maintenance of his consumption goods, i.e., that people do not expend any part of their income on buying maintenance services. This assumption was made for the sake of simplicity. If we alter it, then the allocation of time will also change. The extent to which the allocation of time is affected will depend on what numerical assumptions we make. Interesting differences in the result, however, are observed only when we begin to study the situation not of the average earner but of high income earners. And since the scope for profitable specialization must in practice be greater in the case of this category, there is good reason to study what forces will determine how the work time of these high income earners is changed.

To illustrate the differences, we can construct another numerical example. We will now assume that the person concerned maintains half of his consumption goods, and that he requires half-an-hour per good for this. For the rest of his maintenance he hires services. In column 1 of Table 2, we have assumed that the higher income earner has a productivity level that is twice as high as the average. He will then need to work half an hour, in order to hire one hour of an average income earner's time. What happens with the time allocation will depend on the changes occurring in both average productivity level and the high earner's own productivity level. In column 2 we have assumed that the person's own productivity is doubled, while the average remains unchanged. On the assumptions made, work time will then decrease. We get the same sort of changes as in Table 1. In column 3, we have assumed instead that the average productivity increases. Work time will then increase. This is because the person's real income has deteriorated. He has to pay more for his services. We get the same results as if we had assumed a decline in productivity in Table 1; this in spite of the fact that the person's own productivity level remains unchanged.

What happens if both levels of productivity change at the same time? This is the interesting case. The answer will depend on how much they change and what proportion of total income the higher income earner devotes to services. If we assume — as in column 3 — that he devotes ⅓ of his income to services (7⅙ in relation to 21⅜) and that the general level of productivity rises by 200 per cent, then the higher income earner's productivity must rise by ⅔ for his situation to remain unchanged. To see what salary increase is needed for the higher income earner to compensate for the increased costs of services and thus preserve the status quo, one multiplies the relevant proportion of his budget by the general increase in productivity. Column 4 has been calculated on this assumption. Total work time, consumption volume, and consumption time — and consequently the person's level of satisfaction — remain unchanged. What has happened is a radical reallocation between the time devoted to acquiring consumption goods for personal consumption and to acquiring goods to use as payment for services.

If the higher income earner's productivity had increased, but increased less than it does from column 3 to column 4, then his real income would have fallen. In spite of his improved productivity, his work time would have risen and his consumption time fallen. His total production would have increased, but his consumption would nonetheless decrease. These circumstances can be of interest in assessing how the working hours of high income earners have changed in reality.

We can see that the high income earner's work time will steadily increase as the result of a certain levelling out of income. We can also observe that his work time will be *longer than that of the average earner*. "Leisure for the masses and toil for the classes," as Tibor Scitovsky has described current changes. In column 4, the work time of the higher income earner is $5\frac{1}{3}$ hours, while the average earner, as we can see in Table 1, has a shorter work time than this at a productivity level of 6 units per hour. This is not due to the higher income earners being work addicts, but to their performing specialized work, in order to be able to reduce the time spent in their own personal work. The sum of work time and time for personal work is, therefore, higher for the average earner than the high income earner. These

TABLE 2

Time allocation of a high income earner or certain assumptions of this earner's productivity and the average productivity level. The high income earner is assumed personally to answer for the maintenance of half the goods included in his consumption. The other numerical assumptions made are the same as in Table 1.

	Levels of Productivity			
	Ego's Productivity Level Expressed in No. of Goods Earned Per Hour of Work			
	2	4	4	$6\frac{2}{3}$
	Average Productivity; Here Given As the Number of Goods X Must Pay to Hire One Hour of an Other Earner's Services			
	1	1	2	6
Work time to buy consumption goods	$5\frac{9}{11}$	$3\frac{13}{17}$	$3\frac{5}{9}$	$2\frac{2}{15}$
Work time to buy services	$1\frac{5}{11}$	$\frac{16}{17}$	$1\frac{7}{9}$	$3\frac{2}{10}$
Total work time	$7\frac{3}{11}$	$4\frac{12}{17}$	$5\frac{1}{3}$	$5\frac{1}{3}$
Time in personal work	$2\frac{10}{11}$	$3\frac{13}{17}$	$3\frac{5}{9}$	$3\frac{5}{9}$
Consumption time	$5\frac{9}{11}$	$7\frac{9}{17}$	$7\frac{1}{9}$	$7\frac{1}{9}$
Total time	16	16	16	16
No. consumption goods in the individual's own consumption	$11\frac{7}{11}$	$15\frac{1}{17}$	$14\frac{2}{9}$	$14\frac{2}{9}$
No. goods as payment for services	$2\frac{10}{11}$	$3\frac{13}{17}$	$7\frac{1}{9}$	$21\frac{1}{3}$
Total production	$14\frac{6}{11}$	$18\frac{14}{17}$	$21\frac{3}{9}$	$35\frac{5}{9}$

circumstances, however, mean that we cannot content ourselves with the usual, rough division into work time and free time when studying the correlation between income bracket and work time.

An account of the different changes occurring in practice in work time will be reserved for various reasons until Chapter XI.

CHAPTER IV

The Decline of Service in the Service Economy

Possessions might take more
from the possessor than they
gave. "If I keep a cow," said
Emerson, "that cow milks me."

H. V. Routh

Two Service Sectors

People and goods need maintenance, and maintenance needs time. We need time to maintain our own bodies. We have to sleep, eat, and clean our teeth. We need time to look after the young, the old, and the sick, i.e., to maintain others. We need time to look after various goods and put them in order. We have to cook, wash clothes, clean the house, and do the garden. We need time also to discharge various financial obligations. We must manage our capital (if we have any), keep books, file income tax returns, and make decisions on what to buy and what not to buy. In practice, it may be difficult to draw a line between consumption time and maintenance time. Eating can be a pleasure, or a form of personal work. In spite of this difficulty, there is a difference between time devoted to enjoying consumption goods and, on the other hand, time devoted to looking after the people who are to enjoy them, and time devoted to maintaining the goods themselves.

We shall not necessarily do all this maintenance work ourselves. There is always the possibility, by specialization, of transferring a number of functions to a commercial service sector. The extent to which this is done in practice will depend on what gains are to be made by such specialization. This, in turn, will depend largely on the individual's level of income. The higher the income one has in relation to the rest of the community, the more profitable it will be to specialize. But even for the average earner, with whom this book is mainly concerned, a certain degree of specialization will be profitable. The affluence of the rich countries has come largely from the division of labor. In the production of goods, the gains to be made in this way are so great that we can assume all such production to be specialized. The gains to be made on the maintenance side, however, are not equally great. A considerable number of such tasks will probably always be performed, even as personal work.

If we try to see why the division of labor is so limited on the maintenance side, we can observe to begin with that, as long as we are in good health, it is easier to perform most of our bodily maintenance for ourselves. Sleep is something which we can hardly get from other people, even if they sometimes seem to show a greater facility in this field. We could conceivably employ someone to clean our teeth, but the advantages of this are not great. *Le roi soleil* himself probably brushed his own teeth, if they were brushed at all. As to maintenance of goods we find that there, too, the advantages of division of labor are restricted by the fact that there is less room for profitable mechanization here than in their production. Unless extensive mechanical equipment is required, people will find it simpler to do their own maintenance work. Such gains as may still be offered by the division of labor will often vanish when we take transport costs into consideration. Even if a tailor is better at sewing on buttons than I am, it may be too complicated to go to him with one shirt. Even if an electrician is better than I am at changing light bulbs, it will take him longer than me, if we allow for his travel to and from my house. Also specialization is often hindered by the difficulty in obtaining a clear picture of the market in which we are to find a suitable person or firm to do the job. Many service jobs arise very irregularly, and it can take longer to find out who is the right person to put on a new roof-tile than to do it oneself. Finally, the profitability of specialization is influenced by the normal form of taxation. If the gains offered by the division of labor are smallest in maintenance, taxation will primarily reduce the volume of those functions transferred to the specialized service sector.

An Increased Need of Services

As the volume of consumption goods increases, requirements for the care and maintenance of these goods also tends to increase. We get bigger houses to clean, bigger gardens to look after, a car to wash, a boat to put up for the winter, and a television set to repair, and have to make more decisions on spending. In the case of bodily maintenance, economic growth cannot have the same direct effect. It is possible, however, that higher incomes can lead indirectly to greater demands for personal care. The growing strains of a more hectic life can increase the requirement for "human servicing." The technological advances that permit economic growth can also mean an increase in life expectancy and a greater demand for care of the aged.

In the numerical example we used in discussing the length of working hours, economic growth was found to produce a marked increase in the time devoted to personal work. This example was based on the assumption that the maintenance time per commodity did not vary as the volume of consumption goods rose. This assumption was intended to stress the importance of the extent to which the maintenance time per product changes. It is highly probable that it does change. The forces that a rise in income will release in this direction are of great interest when we study how the quality and quantity of maintenance are influenced by economic growth.

The Quality of Maintenance

Changes in the average maintenance per product will be determined by the sector in which productivity is increasing most rapidly. If the productivity increase is higher in the production of goods than in services, then maintenance will become increasingly expensive in relation to goods. In this situation it will pay to reduce the maintenance per product and instead devote a corresponding amount of time to highly productive work that will offer income to replace the goods that needed service. This is the "use-and-throw-away" system. The maintenance per item is reduced to a level where we only perform service when the yield on the effort corresponds with the level of hourly earnings in specialized work. If productivity were instead to increase more rapidly in the service sector than in production, we should get the converse result. It will then pay to reduce our work time and prolong the maintenance time per commodity.

The case we have most cause to interest ourselves in is a reduction in service time per item as the result of a slower productivity increase in the service sector. This will mean a deterioration in the quality of maintenance provided. Is such a deterioration possible from the technical point of view? In ordinary production there exist, without doubt, situations in which it seems impossible to cut down the service per goods. We cannot, for instance, reduce the maintenance given to aircraft, without regrettable consequences. It is probable, however, that maintenance time varies more in consumption than in production. One reason for this is that a lot of maintenance serves only to increase the pleasure in using goods, not to ensure their technical performance. We wash the car to make it look nice, not to keep it in working order. It is entirely possible to cut down on this sort of maintenance if we like.

Even when the object of maintenance is to get consumption goods to function technically — as with greasing a car — there are still wide margins in the amount of possible service per product. There are two reasons for this. To begin with, the amount of service required often depends on how old the goods are. Service increases with the age of the goods. If, therefore, we discard goods earlier, they will need less service. This must apply even to such sensitive objects as aircraft. Secondly, we can choose to cut down on maintenance, if this will only mean that the goods in question wear out more quickly and have to be replaced sooner. When service costs show a relative increase, one can draw up a new maintenance plan with less service in the initial phase and earlier reprocurement.

Thus openings definitely exist for reducing the quality of maintenance. Such reductions, however, will have a very different effect on the pleasure derived from different goods. The reduced maintenance of certain goods will render them less enjoyable, while with other goods, the amount of pleasure they give will not be affected. It is, therefore, probable that the servicing requirements of different goods will influence the structure of consumption as incomes rise. The man about to buy a large house may hesitate at the thought of the relative rise that will later occur in cleaning costs. When we calculate how the demand for· different goods is dependent on the level of income, we must bear in mind that the relative prices of the goods, owing to discrepancies in the service they require, will necessarily change as incomes rise. (This must be borne in mind in economic theory, in which it is customary, when investigating the correlation between income and demand, to assume that the relative prices of goods are constant.)

Products are also designed with a view to the shifts occurring in the price of maintenance. It is interesting to note that this occurs in two diametrically opposed ways. Either one can make very cheap, simple goods which can be discarded before they require any service, or else one can make specially high quality products that need no service. Both methods are designed to save maintenance time.

If it becomes relatively more expensive to provide maintenance services, then one reduces the maintenance per product. Will the same thing also apply in the case of human servicing? This is doubtful. The reason for cutting down on the maintenance of goods is, after all, that one can, to some extent, substitute reprocurement for maintenance. No such possibility exists in the case of the human body. For this reason, people may want to devote a higher proportion of their growing incomes to increased physical care, the better to enjoy possession of their own, more or less irreplaceable bodies. The scope of this type of service may thus actually increase. Such an income effect, however, could never assert itself with respect to the maintenance of goods, since there it both pays, and is technically possible, to substitute goods for services.

We have now considered what will happen *if* the costs of service rise in relation to the price of goods. What is the case in practice? What prices are in fact showing a relative increase? The answer will depend on where productivity is increasing more rapidly, and this is extremely difficult to decide. Victor Fuchs has made a series of studies on the development of productivity in commercial services. He guards himself with suitable reservations about the uncertainty of his material, but even so ventures to adopt what seems a very clear position. He believes there to be every indication that productivity is rising much more slowly in the service sector than in the production of goods. There is good reason to suppose that one would obtain similar results, if one studied personal work and the development of productivity. Under these circumstances, one could draw the conclusion that a reduction must have been made in maintenance time per item, and that the quality of service has consequently declined.

That development has been faster in production proper than in services does not, of course, mean that productivity in the services sector has not increased. Technical advances make it possible to maintain and service a given item in a shorter time than previously. Plastic boats, for instance, save the boat owner a great deal of work and worry in the spring and autumn. The maintenance work of the housewife has been simplified by dishwashers and vacuum cleaners. Motor-powered lawn mowers make a noise, but undoubtedly reduce the time it takes to keep a lawn trim. Electric shavers perhaps reduce the time spent on our morning toilet. And who, in this context, will not think immediately of the electric beater as an aid in the mixing of dry martinis? Speed reading is another interesting phenomenon. Many of us have felt the urge to develop our reading power by answering one of the advertisements and taking a course. As the skeptics realize, however, rapid comprehension depends on intelligence and motivation, qualities that are not easily procured. Even so, our initial positive reaction to such an idea reveals what we would like to achieve.

There is no doubt that productivity increases have been noted in personal work. But when trying to assess their scale, we must remember that the various mechanical aids involved themselves require time for servicing and that they claim work time to earn money for their purchase. If we fail to remember this, we can easily exaggerate the savings in time that such machines permit. When buying a machine designed to reduce maintenance time, it is easy to ignore the service which that machine will require. The time it takes, for instance, to get an appliance ready for use is sometimes so great that it would pay to do the job by hand. The mechanical shoe polisher often lies unused, because it is quicker to pick up a decent, old-fashioned brush and get on with it. The small scale of operations in the household often makes it difficult to save time by mechanization.

The productivity increase occurring in personal work is, therefore, less than we might think at first sight. We find direct support for this conclusion in a sociological study by J. N. Morgan, T. A. Sirageldin, and F. N. Baerwaldt, which notes that "there is no apparent tendency for the family with more automatic home appliances to spend less time on household activities." There could be various explanations for this, and one of them, at any rate, can be the one we have pointed out. Even so, productivity in personal work has probably undergone a gradual increase. The relative increase in the expensiveness of services has thus been less than it would otherwise have been. The deterioration in the quality of services has proceeded more slowly than it would otherwise have done.

The relative development of costs is of interest in deciding whether there has in fact been any reduction in maintenance per item and, if so, in deciding just how far the quality of maintenance has deteriorated. The absolute change in productivity in personal work is also important in determining how the general scarcity of time has developed. We can then establish — contrary to what we might have thought at first — that, if productivity in personal work has increased, then this has increased the shortage of time. With respect to changes in the scarcity of time, there cannot exist any difference between productivity increases in specialized work and in personal work. If productivity in personal work is rising, then total incomes have risen. This increases the demand for time. The reason why it is commonly thought that these productivity increases in personal work in some way liberate time and reduce the scarcity is that we imagine that the time previously spent in personal work can now be cut down, and that the time saved will be free time. This is a misleading way of looking at it. The time saved will necessarily be distributed over different sectors of use in such a way that the yield on time is everywhere the same. Increased productivity in personal work must lead to time being so allocated that, on the margin, it acquires the same productivity in other sectors. The scarcity of time increases.

Quantity of Maintenance

However, changes also occur in the quantity of maintenance. The scope of total personal work depends, among other things, on the degree of specialization. If an increased amount of service is performed in the commercial service sector, this will tend to decrease the scope of personal work. But such shifts in the one direction or the other do not influence the total amount of maintenance, only *where* the maintenance is performed. We can also note that higher incomes do not in themselves influence the degree of spcialization. Such changes must have their foundation in relative changes in productivity in personal work, in relation to the commercial sector.

More important than changes in the degree of specialization is the effect of reduction in maintenance per product on total maintenance time. We should note, to begin with, that reductions in quality do not necessarily imply reductions in quantity. If the volume of goods to be maintained increases more rapidly than the maintenance per goods decreases, then obviously *total* personal work will increase. It is difficult to state a priori what will happen in practice. If we assume that the proportion between total work time in the production of goods and total time in personal work is constant, and that productivity increases more rapidly in the production of goods, then this means that the production of services in relation to the production of goods tends toward zero. The volume of services is constant, but the volume of goods is increasing. A constant number of hours in personal work would thus mean a drastic decline in the quality of maintenance. If we want to keep up the proportion of services, then time spent in personal work must increase in relation to work time proper. If we should actually want to keep the production of services constant, in relation to the production of goods — an unchanged quality of maintenance — then work time, in relation to service time, would tend toward zero, as we saw in Table 1. This relationship has been formulated in an interesting paper by Baumol.

How the scope of personal work has developed in practice does not appear to have been studied. One thing we do know is that economic growth has always been accompanied by an increasing proportion of employees in the commercial service sector. In the United States, the service sector is the only sector to have increased its relative proportion of employees in the postwar period. Unless this is due entirely to changes in the degree of specialization, there should have been a corresponding increase in total personal work. At least one sociologist, V. W. Bladen, believes this to be the case, and he has expressed his view very strikingly. He claims:

. . . that a little leisure is likely to be spent with a view to recovery from fatigue: that a lot of leisure is likely to be spent in strenuous activity inducing fatigue; and that one particular form of this activity deserving study is the second job; another is the do it yourself work in your house. Is it too fantastic to picture Monday as the day on which men recover at work from the fatigue of a strenuous Saturday and Sunday?

The Decline of Service in the Service Economy

Thus it seems that a process of economic development involves both an increase in the quantity of service and a decline in the quality. Many, of course, have noted the increase occurring in the relative number of persons employed in the commercial service sector. The conclusion has been drawn that we are enjoying a general improvement in services. It has been ignored that the decisive factor for a high standard of service is the service item rather than the total volume of services. A deterioration in the *quality* of service perhaps provides a better description of existence in the rich countries than the increase in *quantity* of service. We have good reason to speak of "the decline of service in the service economy."

CHAPTER V

Short Cuts in Private and Public Services

... it is also imprudent to fall sick or die
between 6:00 p.m. on a Friday evening and 9:00 a.m.
on a Monday morning. If you fall sick between
those hours, you may get no medical attention;
and, if, in consequence, you die, you will certainly
not be able to get yourself buried till Monday
comes. Translate this meticulous two days' blackout
into a five days' one, and you have the world
of the future ... Even if the workers' two-day
stints are staggered to cover all seven days of
the week, they will cover them so thinly that the
affluent world will still be a most inconvenient
and uncomfortable world to live in.

Arnold J. Toynbee

Personal Care and Maintenance

Let us take some examples to show how a reduced quality of services has already altered our existence. Obviously, people have different preferences and react differently to the need to economize their time: the ways in which they cut down on maintenance will thus vary. But the pattern will be the same. With varying degrees of alacrity we are all travelling along paths which lead to less time being available for each of the different kinds of maintenance.

As regards care of our own persons, we can note, to begin with, that many people regard sleep as a waste of time. The greater the demand for time, the more people come to accept this view. Some have actually tried systematically to cut down the number of hours thus spent in passivity. Only limited success has been met in this field, but we have succeeded in abolishing the luxury of the afternoon nap. Even children no longer sleep in the afternoon. But as regards a sound night's sleep, we can cut down on the number of hours only for brief periods without nature taking her revenge. Hopes for further progress in this respect are often expressed. Godfrey M. Lebhar reminds us that if we slept only a half-hour less per day, this would correspond over a whole lifetime to a total of two years. He believes that it would be possible, after a number of initial difficulties, to reduce one's need for sleep. Morris Ernst, who paints a rosy picture of life in 1976, has the following to say about sleep: "About a third of these [168 weekly hours] are presently needed for sleep. This figure may be much reduced as we approach the less tense and more satisfying way of living in 1976. Experiments indicate that under relaxed and satisfying habits six hours will be enough to replenish our bodily energies."

While waiting for 1976, we find ourselves in an entirely different situation. It seems as if our hectic daylight lives make it increasingly difficult to utilize the hours set aside for rest. Many are the victims of insomnia. The same hectic pressure of life then cruelly squeezes the sufferer from bed in the morning. To an increasing extent, people are resorting to drugs to combat the insomnia that threatens to make their nights unproductive. Sales of sleeping pills are rising.

As an alternative to cutting down the number of hours we spend asleep, there is the hope of exploiting this virgin time for something useful. Specifically, the possibility has been broached of absorbing knowledge during sleep. Students would very much like to be able to absorb knowledge by tape recorder, without having to wake up. Business executives would surely like to have financial reports played into their memories during the night. Sleep, it seems, has something in common with the recreation areas in our big cities: both are subject to continual attacks from those who would like to use these resources for productive purposes.

What of our personal hygiene? Washing takes time. Some people perhaps feel it is their duty to compromise on occasion, to have a few dirty minutes. Some people use deodorants the way people in less hygiene-conscious ages used perfume — as an alternative to washing. One advertisement explains that vaginal douches take time and are a nuisance and proposes instead that women use disinfectant suppositories. A background to this exhortation is provided by a wedding photograph, newlyweds with happy smiles.

Who has time to follow the dentist's advise to clean our teeth after every meal? It is quicker to fill the unbrushed cavities at regular intervals. Some people use delays in the traffic, in order to shave in the car. On the whole, many people let their entire apparatus — clothes, hair, shoes, etc. — present a markedly uncared-for appearance, not because they lack money, but because they are in a hurry. *The Other America,* according to Michael Harrington, is not so noticeable, because the poor in a country like the United States, with its highly mechanized textile industry, can afford relatively decent clothes. "America has the best-dressed poverty the world has ever known." This may be true, but the lack of contrast afforded by the poor is also due to those with money devoting so little time to their appearance. Some of the students I have seen in the United States must have gained several months towards their doctorates in this way. One can travesty Harrington and say: "America has the least well-dressed affluence the world has ever known."

We have no time to cook food. Actual cooking is a time-consuming process, and has been abandoned for thawing and heating, which is not an unqualified advance. We have made the transition from appetizing food to acceptable nutrition. The bookshelves of American department stores, where only best sellers are permitted to compete for space, contain such titles as the *I Hate to Cook Book, The No Cooking Cookbook, The 10 Minute Gourmet Cookbook,* and *The Instant Epicure Cookbook for Terribly Tired Gourmets.* There is also another category: the expensive, richly illustrated thick volume that hopeful husbands buy to advance an argument which the recipient will never have time to read.

In any case, we have no time to eat either. It is a vicious circle. Poor food inclines us to reduce the time spent at the table to below the level necessitated by the pressure of time, and this in its turn makes it even less attractive to spend time on preparing well-cooked meals. We have reached a stage at which some people actually eat their lunch standing up. A number of restaurants — particularly, as we might expect, in New York — encourages this arrangement as a means of increasing turnover. The fact that this is acceptable, shows the state we have reached. The degeneration of the arts of cooking and eating seems likely to alter the face of living even in Lucullan, France. Parisian lunch tables have already suffered from the centrifugal forces radiating from modern customers and the modern cuisine. We certainly sin against the ninth aphorism of Brillat-Savarin: "The discovery of a new dish contributes more to the happiness of mankind than the discovery of a new star."

While on the subject of food, let us not forget how our waistlines spread as the time available for exercise shrinks. American cinema owners have reportedly been forced to broaden the seats in cinemas not simply for the comfort of filmgoers but actually to enable them to get their behinds down. Obesity, as we know, is a major health problem in the wealthy countries of the world. If we have numerous hospitals, it is partly because we lack the time to avoid the necessity of hospitalization.

All this means that we are neglecting the maintenance of our bodies — a machine like all other machines — in our attempts to gain time. But sleeping less, eating more quickly, taking less exercise, and washing more quickly — all these are only short-term savings in time. The presssure that results from all other changes in the use of time probably makes it increasingly important, medically, that we relax by sound sleep, unhurried mealtimes, and pleasant walks. To judge from the obituary notices in *The New York Times,* many young executives seem to have adopted a maintenance schedule on their own bodies that provides for rapid wear and little initial maintenance, i.e., the principle for the maintenance of goods that we formulated in Chapter IV. To find less superficial statistical methods of illustrating the correlation between income and life expectancy, we can consult various studies made in recent years. These show that income is negatively correlated with life expectancy, but that higher incomes permit the earners to purchase more and better medical care, thus compensating for the menacing effect of the income increases themselves. Income increases lead to a deterioration in health, which is then propped up by medicine and hospital care. These results are observed, in spite of the fact that the high earners of the world initially probably have a stronger than average physical constitution.

The surprising negative correlation between state of health and income can be confirmed by the following quotation from a report by Victor F. Fuchs, in which he sums up various empirical investigations:

The prevailing assumption, in some cases with good evidence, has indicated that an increase in real per capita income has favorable implications for health, apart from the fact that it permits an increase in health services. This assumption for the United States at present, except for infant mortality, may reasonably be questioned. This country may have passed the peak with respect to the favorable impact of a rising level of living on health. This is not to say that some favorable elements are not still associated with a higher income, but the many unfavorable ones may outweigh them.

More Examples: Child Care and Number of Children

The bringing up of children is partly a pleasure, partly a maintenance job. Are we trying to save time here, too? Have we perhaps reduced the maintenance time per child?

In a number of families, the trend is probably to devote an increasing amount of time to care of the children. There are signs, however, that many other families have instead reduced the amount of attention devoted to their children. A widely advertised book, published in 1966, has the revealing title: *How to Raise Children at Home in Your Spare Time*. Regardless of the content of this manual, it is significant that both the author and the publishers clearly considered it a selling proposition that the road to success in child raising is not necessarily a long one.

It is not unusual to hear busy fathers regretting the fact that they never get around to meeting their children. William Whyte quotes such a case in *The Organization Man*. "I sort of look forward to the days my kids are grown up," one sales manager said. "Then I won't have to have such a guilty conscience about neglecting them." It may be that statements of this type do not imply any absolute reduction in the time devoted to children, but reflect rather a more widespread view that fathers *should* get to know their children. The fact remains that people are prevented by the pressure of time from performing what has come to be regarded as an important duty in the care of children.

Also, children are being left to a greater extent to outside care in nurseries, even at a very early age. It is difficult to decide whether or not this is a good thing for the children. It is sufficient for our purposes to note that the children are farmed out, largely in order to reduce the time spent on their care. We can perhaps also recall the various anecdotes in circulation about parents who purchase exemption from one or another duty by means of coins pressed into the child's hand. This method accurately reflects the pattern of adjustment analyzed in the present study: money is substituted for time. In the old days, parents spanked their children. Now they would like to caress them, but lack the time. Every age has its drawbacks.

It is not only the time spent per child but also the actual number of children that can be affected by income increases. The correlation between number of children and level of income has been widely discussed. The conventional doctrine is that the number of children declines as level of income rises. "The poor only get children." More recent studies show that this is perhaps due only to discrepancies in familiarity with birth-control techniques. We can say in this case that the number of *wanted* children increases, as incomes rise.

That increases in income should have such a positive effect on the number of children is thought to agree with the theory of demand in economics, in which the income effect is usually considered to be positive. When making studies of this type, however, one must also bear in mind the different claims on time made by different ways of using money. Insofar as children make greater claims on time than, say, various goods, this will tend to reduce the number of children. It is a question of which is the stronger: the income effect, as such, or the changed cost relationships arising from the increase in income. We must not forget that the cost structure changes with increases in income. No abstracted effect of income exists in practice, owing to the differing claims on time made by different utilities.

What we might expect is that the altered cost relationships would have a particularly strong effect in cases where the wife enjoys a high income. That this is the case has in fact been demonstrated by Mincer, in an empirical study.

Children, however, do not only claim time. They can also be said to increase the supply of time within a family. In the old days, people often regarded children as an investment that would yield interest when the children could be put to productive work. They could then increase the supply of goods in the family. It may be that people are now behaving as if children were a *time investment*. This investment would then begin to yield an interest when the children reached an age at which they required less time in care than they provided in consumption time. In this way, children would have the same significance as an increase in the labor strength of an industrial plant. The children would permit an increase in the manufacture of pleasure. Someone has observed that many executives have no time really to enjoy their high incomes, but that they can at least have the satisfaction of knowing that their stand-ins on the home front are vicariously devoting themselves to all manner of consumption.

The Problem of Old Age

Economic growth has in one respect dramatically reduced our life expectancy: we no longer feel the same need to imagine a life free from material cares in the hereafter. Belief in an eternal life has thus declined. On the other hand, the average life expectancy on this planet has been prolonged by medical advances. It may be — as suggested above — that further income increases in the rich countries are reducing the life expectancy, but the situation, compared with a century ago, is still clear. To some extent this increased life expectancy is due to a lesser mortality rate in the early years, but there has still been a considerable decrease in mortality in the higher age groups.

The latter type of increased life expectancy is bound to present certain difficulties, which stem from an increasing shortage of maintenance time. At an advanced age, the body — like the fuselage of an elderly aircraft — requires a great deal of maintenance, in order to function. We scrap old cars, but hang on to old bodies. The instinct of self-preservation means that in this one case we do everything we can to preserve a "possession" that makes extremely high demands for maintenance. In other cases, we try systematically to rid ourselves of such possessions. This is an interesting example of a failure in our efforts to dispense with items requiring excessive maintenance.

A person of advanced age requires not so much the spectacular repairs in which modern medicine excels, as it requires personal attention, and daily routine care. The need for attention is strengthened by the fact that the individual is often incapable of providing even the bodily care that people normally give themselves. The free play for technical advances in this respect is very limited. It is, therefore, hardly surprising if old people are exposed to the active generation's efforts to cut down the amount of service per "unit." As average income rises, increased efforts will be made to cut down on the attention given to the old, per individual.

Growing old in a wealthy country is a mixed pleasure. The wheel has turned full circle. Previously, productivity was low and the scarcity of goods accordingly great. For this reason, it was often impossible to support the old. The *"attestupa"* or suicidal precipice of the Vikings was the historical solution in Scandinavia. Nowadays, productivity is high, and time consequently so scarce that only a few people will sacrifice the time needed to care adequately for the old and infirm. Previously there were too few goods, now there is too little time. It is, therefore, hardly surprising that we are experiencing a crisis in the care of old people and are discussing how it will be possible to maintain the traditional criteria of death and, at the same time, provide attention that can be described as "humane."

Public Services in the Affluent Society

Public services, like other services, are subject to only a limited amount of efficiency engineering. If Parkinson's law is valid, the development of productivity in this sector is actually negative. This means that public services are becoming relatively more and more expensive. It would be surprising if this did not mean a gradual deterioration of service. Total *expenditure* on public services per capita may be increasing, but the *volume* of many services is probably declining.

Certain public services, however, are more in the nature of investments. Education and training are an investment in human capital. Here the volume may very well be increased in our efforts to accelerate economic growth. The risks are greater in the case of such education as does not appear to be occupational. The explosion in education has hardly affected such subjects as philosophy and ancient history. Another service that in many countries is of a public nature is medical care. Here again, it is largely a question of investment. We prevent a human capital from being consumed. In the care of old people, which does not have this effect, the situation is in a much more vulnerable position.

Many public services, however, are not in the nature of investments, and it is probable that their quality will steadily deteriorate. An example is the mail system. Here, an apparently continuous decline in service is taking place. The number of weekdays on which mail is delivered has declined, as has the number of deliveries per day. In the United States, one hears astonishing reports of how long it can take for letters to reach their destination. These reports stem not only from the general public, but from the mail authorities themselves. It is not uncommon for mail to be left unsorted at the post office for several days. The introduction of the zip code implies another kind of decline in service, requiring people to take time to look up postal numbers when writing an address.

Another example is the cleaning of roads and streets, and snow clearance. In the absence of any figures, I must rely on my own scattered observations, which again suggest a steady deterioration in quality. The same seems to apply to the police force. Crime is increasing, but the resources of the police services are not keeping up. Consequently, a declining amount of attention is devoted to each offense. This circumstance is to some extent concealed by the fact that large resources are deployed to solving crimes which attract the attention of the news media. Reports made on other offenses are usually filed and forgotten. In a Swedish daily paper in the fall of 1967, a superintendent of police expressed the following opinion, after 35 years in the service: "I am simply ashamed. It is impossible today to do a proper job of police work. Our work is shoddy, and and the people who have more than a casual interest in crime know it." A contributory cause of the rising proportion of unsolved crimes must be the higher relative cost of maintaining a police force.

The circumstance that the rich countries usually provide poor quality public activities has been forcibly pointed out by J. K. Galbraith in *The Affluent Society.*

Further Examples: The Maintenance of Material Things

Material resources of various kinds have probably been exposed more than anything else to a growing lack of care and maintenance. The reason is that there exists such an evident possibility of using time to acquire new goods, instead of maintaining the old, and winning on the deal as productivity in manufacturing rises. Homes are less well cared for, the layers of dust become a bit more noticeable. We wash the car a bit less regularly and, if we have two cars, even less regularly. Boats are not as well cared for as they used to be. A golfer not playing in a competition spends less time looking for the ball that he has sliced into the rough, nor does he keep his clubs in the shape their high quality invites. Records are left out of their covers and not dusted before use. We acquire more and more leisure articles, but each of them is less well kept. Tennis rackets are left lying out in the rain, if we "haven't the time" to take them in. Food is wasted, to avoid bothering about how to use leftovers. Lost-and-found departments find that fewer and fewer people come to look for their umbrellas.

Behavior of the type exemplified here often means a standard of hygiene lower than we would like to believe, owing to the decline in maintenance. We have already observed that personal hygiene is sometimes subject to compromise. We have also claimed that the cleaning of our towns has deteriorated. Finally, we have now seen that many of our belongings can get fairly dirty before we bother to do anything about it. It may be that economic growth in the rich countries leads to a rising standard of how clean things *should* be, while in fact everything is getting dirtier. Only in the initial phase of economic growth will awareness of the importance of hygiene lead to a rising standard of actual cleanliness. When incomes have reached a certain level, further increases will lead to our towns, our parks, our homes, our bodies, the air we breathe and the lungs we breathe it with, the food we eat, and the water we drink becoming ever more polluted. In the field of hygiene, we practice a double system of morality. To adhere to the one we preach would be too expensive.

How We Manage Our Financial Assets

The cavalier manner in which it pays to manage our possessions applies also to our financial assets. The higher average income rises, the more marked this behavior becomes. This observation holds true in a time series study, but not necessarily in a cross-section analysis. It is often said that no one is as careful about spending money as a rich man. This may be true, since those with higher incomes can be in this position just because they do devote great attention to private economic matters. However, the average earner, when average income rises, behaves more and more carelessly in economic affairs.

To take an example, it is noticeable how people are becoming increasingly disinterested in counting their change. Of more consequence perhaps is the fact that people, as their incomes rise, have a greater propensity for keeping liquid funds on hand, in order to save time. If it cost nothing to obtain cash when one needed it, then people would keep all their money in a form that earned interest. In fact, it costs money to liberate funds. To begin with, the bank may exact a payment for each transaction. But what is of interest for our purposes is that it costs time for the person in question to have a sum of money translated into liquid form. He has to telephone or visit the bank, and order the transaction in question. These costs are bound to affect our behavior.

William Baumol has shown that these costs must be weighed against the loss of interest, and that they will determine the amount of cash the individual will keep on call. The higher the costs, the more liquid funds will be kept on hand. However, when Baumol goes on to discuss how changes in interest rates affect the size of the funds kept on call, he assumes that these costs are constant. He never even discusses how they might be thought to change. To ignore this factor may be a legitimate simplification. It is worth pointing out that the costs in fact are not constant, but depend entirely on how expensive the individual's time is. In a recession time becomes cheaper and the funds kept on hand tend to become relatively smaller for this reason. A greater proportion of money is kept in a form that attracts interest. If the interest rate is cut, then this will reduce, *ceteris paribus,* the advantages of keeping money where it attracts interest. And if the cut in interest rates stimulates levels of business so that incomes rise, then the costs of maintaining nonliquid funds will also rise. These are circumstances that should perhaps be analyzed and incorporated into theories of monetary policy.

For the majority of people, however, the question of how they handle their purchases is more important than how they manage their assets. Shopping is a very time-consuming activity. Empirical studies show that housewives, for instance, spend a considerable amount of time in shops, and en route to and from shops. At certain periods of the year, we have all spent so much time in shopping that these labors occupy a prominent place in our consciousness. This applies particularly to the Christmas rush. An American shipping line has observed our frustration and runs the following advertisement: "Aren't the two weeks before Christmas the worst of the year? Not if you do your Christmas shopping here," i.e., on a cruise to the tropics.

The promise of "money returned if not to full satisfaction" is often made probably in the knowledge that customers will not bother to take the time to return the goods, even if they are dissatisfied. The higher the level of incomes, the more goods fail to be returned.

The time it takes to go shopping must also be borne in mind when assessing the probable future scale of the throw-away system. It will probably put a powerful brake on the spread of this system. A further limitation can be seen in the scale of the end service required by the throw-away system, in the form of garbage disposal costs.

The most important way in which consumers can reduce the time required to shop is to limit the time spent in thinking about what to buy. As incomes rise, less and less time is devoted on the average to each decision. One comes to rely on increasingly rough rules of thumb. This will apply to all types of economic decisions, even those relating to the management of financial assets. Reduced time for reflection previous to a decision would apparently entail a growing irrationality. However, since it is extremely rational to consider less and less per decision, there exists a rationale of irrationality. The important questions arising from the deteriorating quality of economic decisions require a chapter of their own.

CHAPTER VI

The Rationale of Growing Irrationality

There are, however, reasons for
the backwardness of the art of
spending money . . .

W. C. Mitchell

The Need for a Decision Theory

Every individual has to make numerous decisions and of different kinds. He has to decide on questions of love and politics, economics and ethics, work and pastimes — on everything that makes up his existence. It is of interest to try to form a picture of how individuals behave in choosing between the different alternatives that face them. To this end, various attempts have been made to formulate theories of decision-making. These differ from each other, according to the assumptions made as to a) the individual's awareness in his attempts to achieve some form of happiness, and b) the individual's knowledge of his alternatives.

Collecting information on the different alternatives available takes time. The time required by decision-making is a particular component in what we have called maintenance time or time for personal work. As the scarcity of time changes, it will probably affect the amount of time allocated to decision-making. This will have considerable consequences, and affords reason to consider what changes in time allocation are conceivable in this context.

The Assumption of Rationality

To be able to make statements relating to economic behavior, it is usual in economics to make the assumption of rationality. This assumption is in two parts. The first relates to the degree of knowledge possessed concerning the different alternatives and their consequences. It is assumed that the person making the decision possesses *complete* knowledge of the different courses of action available, and that this knowledge is acquired without any particular cost. Secondly, rationality means the assumption of a complete system of preferences, so that the decision-maker can place the different alternatives in rank order. He is then supposed to select the alternative that heads the list.

With such an assumption of rationality, it is possible to describe decision-making in economic questions — and in other questions that could conceivably be approached in the same way — as a problem of maximization. Consumers, producers, and politicians will maximize their pleasure, their profit, and their prospects of reelection.

Obviously, economists regard the assumption of rationality as a simplification. No one claims that it presents a complete or even adequate picture of reality. All theories are based on simplifying assumptions, designed to reduce the task to manageable proportions. This is why the economists have chosen to make the assumption of rationality; it is thought to serve as a manageable approximation of the truth.

Attacks and Reformulations

Outside the ranks of the economists, the assumption of rationality is probably regarded with great skepticism. The psychologists, for instance, will hardly be impressed by such a simple construction. Even some of those employed in economic analysis — and who have, therefore, been faced with the necessity of making simplifying assumptions — have been critical. The view has been put forward that the rationality assumption means ignoring many interesting questions entirely, and giving an inadequate answer to others.

Those criticizing the economists have chosen different points of attack. Some have rejected the idea of the well-ordered system of preferences, within which a decision-maker can rank his alternatives and select the best. The forcible wording of Th. Veblen's frontal attack on "the economic man" has made it perhaps the best known.

The hedonistic conception of man is that of a lightning calculator of pleasures and pains, who oscillates like a homogeneous globule of desire of happiness under the impulse of stimuli that shift him about the area, but leave him intact. He has neither antecedent nor consequent. He is an isolated, definitive human datum, in stable equilibrium except for the buffets of the impinging forces that displace him in one direction or another. Self-imposed in elemental space, he spins symmetrically about his own spiritual axis until the parallelogram of forces bears down upon him, whereupon he follows the line of the resultant. When the force of the impact is spent, he comes to rest, a self-contained globule of desire as before. Spiritually, the hedonistic man is not a prime mover. He is not the seat of a process of living, except in the sense that he is subject to a series of permutations enforced upon him by circumstances external and alien to him.

This criticism, made in 1898, may or may not be justified. It is worth emphasizing, however, that it has at least not become antiquated as the result of any subsequent alteration to the basic assumptions of economic theory.

A group of economists with close ties to psychology has rejected the idea that everyone has a complete knowledge of his alternatives. The leader of this school is Herbert A. Simon, who considers that information is not available gratis and has to be acquired by search. Alternatives are discovered and investigated, but hardly in accordance with any complete system that guarantees optimal results. The actual order in which one examines different alternatives has a major influence on subsequent action. One stops at an alternative that is judged to be satisfactory in relation to the ambition level when adopted or, as the term is, "satisficing." The procession of search can be continued, in order gradually to find superior alternatives. One will always, however, act from inadequate knowledge, particularly as external circumstances are gradually changing and altering the advantages and drawbacks of the respective alternatives.

Another school of critics is concerned not with rejecting the assumption of rationality, but rather with modifying it. They have tried to allow for the fact that some degree of uncertainty must always prevail regarding the outcome of different alternative actions. To the extent that those making the decisions can attach various probabilities to the different outcomes, it is still possible to handle decisions as problems of maximization. Decision-makers maximize their mathematical expectation of achieving the targets set. Insofar as they are ignorant of the probabilities valid for different alternatives, they are forced to resort to various strategies that can guarantee the avoidance of major risks in their choice.

Apart from allowing for a perhaps inevitable degree of uncertainty, these critics have also pointed out that the uncertainty can be reduced by collecting information. The uncertainty relating to the different alternatives is not externally given. But — and this is what they want us to take into account — increased knowledge can be acquired only at a price. This cost must be weighed against the value of the greater knowledge acquired. This is a typical problem of allocation. The object is to state the equilibrium condition — in this case for the amount of information gathering to be performed. Information is to be sought up to a point, at which further knowledge would cost more than it is worth.

The difference between these decision-makers and Simon's "satisficers" is greater than may appear at first sight. In Simon's system, one meets decision-makers who are engaged in a process in which they successively investigate alternatives, using the one that best fulfills certain basic criteria until they have found a superior alternative. Those, on the other hand, who are concerned with the costs and receipts of information are not interested in the possible bearing of the actual process of search on the solutions tested. The picture instead is that, previous to a decision, one acquires information on all alternatives, so far as this pays off, and then chooses the best alternative. In fact, there is no real contradiction between these two approaches. To allow for the costs of information is a first step, which should perhaps be followed by also allowing for the setting up of the actual search program. The assumptions made will depend on the type of problems we are concerned with investigating.

It is clear, however, that even such a minor modification as allowing for the costs of information will help us to understand many phenomena that have their roots in the ignorance actually prevailing, and necessarily prevailing even in optimal conditions. In his attack on the rationality assumption, George Stigler expresses this thought in a striking manner:

> Ignorance is like subzero weather: by a sufficient expenditure its effects upon people can be kept within tolerable or even comfortable bounds, but it would be wholly uneconomic entirely to eliminate all its effects. And, just as an analysis of man's shelter and apparel would be somewhat incomplete if cold weather is ignored, so also our understanding of economic life will be incomplete if we do not systematically take account of the cold winds of ignorance.

Scarcity of Time and the Quality of Decisions

If we keep to the more limited target of allowing for information costs, then we at once face the question of how far these costs are changed and how far this affects the quality of the decisions made by individuals. Only one economist, Jacob Mincer, seems to have considered this problem. As the individual's income rises, the costs of each hour devoted to acquiring information increase. If there is no productivity increase in information gathering, the cost of attaining a certain level of knowledge will rise precisely as much as the increase in real wages in production. But, Mincer goes on, the advantages of possessing information also increase as income rises, and will in fact increase in step with income. Each error now relates to a large sum of money. If incomes are doubled, then it is twice as profitable to avoid making a given error in expenditure. On the average, an unchanged amount of information gathering will, therefore, be performed. This, however, as Mincer points out, will not prevent changes in the degree of knowledge occurring with respect to different goods. If expenditure on a certain product increases less than in proportion to income, then the advantages of acquiring information will increase less than the costs. The process of search will be curtailed. If, on the other hand, expenditure increases more than in proportion, then the advantages of possessing information on these goods will increase more than in proportion with the costs. More information will then be acquired. In other words, the quality of expenditure decisions relating to goods with an income elasticity above 1 will be improved. The quality of expenditure decisions relating to goods with an income elasticity below 1 will deteriorate. One will thus consider more carefully such expenditure as relates to luxury goods, but reflect less carefully on expenditure relating to the necessities.

Mincer also points out that the advantages of specialization mean that the costs of acquiring information will not increase as rapidly as income. A high income earner will profit by buying information rather than devoting his own time to the acquisition of all information.

The conclusions of Mincer's analysis are thus that the average quality of expenditure decisions will, if anything, increase as the level of income rises, but that interesting differences will emerge among goods, depending on how sensitive the demand is to income. Mincer's discussion, however, is open to certain objections. To begin with, an increase in the average level of income will not automatically mean that one can keep down the increase in information costs by specializing and buying information. Only when one's own income rises in relation to others can one, in this way, profit from employing others to collect information on a larger scale. Since it is our present task to see what happens when the average income rises, we can ignore these advantages of specialization.

Secondly, there is reason to question the view that the advantages of possessing information will increase in step with the costs of acquiring it. If total expenditure rises more slowly than the costs per hour — which would be the case with a reduction in working hours — then the receipts from possessing information increases less rapidly than the costs. The advantages of information depend on total expenditure, while the costs of information depend on the hourly wage. Also, Mincer's idea that information costs do not increase more than the advantages is based on an assumption that the total number of decisions remains unchanged. Only in such circumstances can the scope of each decision increase in step with the costs of planning the decision in question. If one imagines instead that each decision relates to an unchanged sum, but that the number of decisions increases as the result of higher incomes, then the advantages of possessing information with respect to a given decision have not increased at all, while the costs of acquiring knowledge have. It is, in fact, extremely probable that an increase in average income is accompanied by an increase in the number of decisions to be taken. The alternatives increase, and it is probable that every individual is concerned with diversifying both his activities and his expenditure, with a view to testing the new openings offered by rising incomes and more advanced technology.

In combination, these forces would mean that the costs of collecting information increased more rapidly than the advantages. Only if there is an increase in productivity in the gathering of information can the rise in information costs be kept down. It is probable that such an increase in productivity has occurred. It must have been particularly noticeable when the general level of education was raised by the introduction and extension of compulsory schooling. More recent increases in levels of education, however, can hardly have had the same importance in these respects, since education at an advanced level is specialized and thus loses its bearing on the ease with which knowledge of the consequences of different decisions can be acquired. There are other ways, too, in which productivity in the collection of information can increase. One example is consumer information. Even so, there seem to be good grounds for assuming that the increase in productivity has been slower here than in the manufacture of goods. This would fit with findings as regards productivity changes in the services sector at large.

In this case, the yield on time spent in acquiring information on different decisions would gradually deteriorate in relation to the yield on time spent in production. This must lead to a reallocation of time. The time used to acquire information must be reduced per decision. One has to concentrate on acquiring information only of such value that the yield on the time spent for this purpose will be as high as in the production of goods. It pays to make a larger number of mistakes in expenditure, instead of preparing all decisions very carefully — and thus having correspondingly less time to acquire income. As the scarcity of time increases, we can expect a decline in the quality of decisions. People will deviate to an increasing extent from the behavior presupposed in economic theory. Instead of possessing complete knowledge, we shall be acting on increasingly uncertain grounds.

The Uninformed Consumer

The requirement that the yield on time must increase as the level of incomes rises is a general one; it relates to time spent on all different purposes, including, as we have seen, in making decisions. And it must apply to the time spent in making all sorts of decisions, not just economic ones. Only half in jest, one can perhaps claim to find examples of a declining quality of decision-making in all possible fields. Is it possible that we devote less and less time to forming our opinions on a life after death? Is it that we spend less and less time thinking of the ultimate purpose of our economic growth? Do we find less and less time to decide our attitudes to various political problems? Do we take a lover without seriously contemplating the factors involved? Obviously the amount of time we spend reflecting on these different questions is influenced also by changes in attitude that occur parallel with rising incomes. We perhaps develop a taste for being well-informed. This difference in attitude will then counteract the force that would in itself lead to our cutting down the time devoted to different decisions.

In the case of economic decisions, such changes in attitude can hardly occur. If it is relatively profitable to raise one's standard of living by working to earn money rather than working to acquire information, then it will obviously pay to substitute work for information-gathering time. It is, therefore, simplest to consider the economic sector, when trying to find examples of the principle of a declining quality of decision-making.

An interesting phenomenon is that purchases are nowadays often made on the impulse of the moment, rather than after careful thought. It appears to be old-fashioned to make lists of intended purchases. People shop as they wander up and down the aisles of the self-service store. They use the store as a giant catalog which shows them what is available. Modern housewives actually seem to compose the week's menus while strolling among the goods on display. J. West, after a two-year study in various Canadian towns, reports that 37 per cent of all purchases can be classified as impulse purchases. This study, reported in 1951, was based on over 5,000 interviews with customers who had purchased a total of 15,500 goods. Even more interesting are the results obtained in a series of investigations by the E. I. du Pont de Nemours & Company over a number of years. As expected, the material shows a marked upswing in unplanned purchases over the years. In 1949, the percentage was 38 per cent, which agrees with the figure reported by West. By 1954 the figure had risen to 48 per cent, and by 1959 it was 50 per cent. Obviously, these percentages depend on what we mean by impulse purchases. But as long as the definitions are not altered, the changes reported would seem to have a basis in reality. The figures do not indicate that people buy a lot of goods they do not want, and which they will never have any use for. They simply show that there has been a marked increase in the number of purchases made without previous careful thought.

When we look specifically at the amount of information acquired previous to the purchase of more expensive products, we find that impulse purchases are less frequent. Here too, however, various studies suggest that the informative material collected before purchase is relatively scanty. Nor is this surprising. There is reason to expect that people will prefer to make an occasional mistake, rather than spend a long time considering each decision.

George Katona and Eva Mueller have made a study designed to illustrate how much information people gather before buying capital consumer goods. The results show that: ". . . only about a fourth of durable goods buyers displayed most of the essential features of deliberate decision making — planning, family discussions, information seeking, as well as choosing with respect to price, brand, and other specific attributes of the commodity."

Those who spent practically no time at all on planning the purchase in question answered for another ones fourth. Those trying most actively to acquire information were to be found in the middle income bracket. Both high and low income earners spent less time on reflection. That the high income earners should have collected less information fits our thesis of a declining quality of decisions. That low income earners should collect relatively little information is in conflict with it. The explanation may be that their low level of education meant a low yield on time spent in the collection of information. What we need is not so much comparisons between income brackets, but comparisons between different points of time with different average incomes. We need a time series analysis rather than a cross-section.

Impulse purchases show that expenditure is not subject to any real reflection. Another indication is the many different rules of thumb employed in acquiring and interpreting information. To take price as an index of quality is sometimes considered the height of human folly. It may be stupid, but it seems less stupid when we take into account that it is a quick method of grading. In actual fact, it may be a very reasonable rule of thumb to equate price with quality. The mistakes made in this way may very well be less expensive than the efforts that would be required to avoid them by acquiring better information. As is clear from the following statement from F. Ölander, behavioral scientists concerned with economics are not strangers to such an idea: "From the psychologist's standpoint, there seems to be no prior reason for belittling the role that price can play in indicating quality to a consumer, who is almost always acting under uncertainty with respect to many of the aspects of the purchasing situation, and who is on the look-out for all kinds of cues that can help him in his decision making."

The authority adopting this attitude quotes also a number of other authors expressing the same opinion.

Another rule of thumb that is often used is to judge the quantity of a product from the size of the packaging. Since the manufacturers are aware of this rule of thumb and make misleading packages, consumers accordingly make numerous mistakes. This, however, does not prevent the consumers from perhaps profiting from the commission of certain limited mistakes, rather than having to making the unlimited efforts that would be required to avoid all erroneous decisions. Some theories of business economics have tried in fact to allow for the way in which the consumers' time situation affects their behavior. This is clear from what Howard, for instance, the author of one of the leading textbooks on marketing theory, has to say. "By time pressures is meant the amount of time available for the decision in relation to the task involved in making the decision: each buyer allocates his scarce time among alternative purchases. He must allocate his total time between purchasing and nonpurchasing activities."

By assuming that time is a resource, and one that is becoming increasingly scarce, it is possible to apply economic theory to systematize what business economists have been able to observe of consumer behavior, and to give content to the economists' theory of consumer behavior. The latter, owing to the assumption of rationality, is at present extremely meager. It covers really only the factors determining how consumers divide their incomes between consumption and saving. It would perhaps be possible to construct various bridges between economics and business economics by replacing the former's rationality assumption with something that allows for the time scarcity and the costs of information. Economists should not find this foreign to them. They themselves make decisions without complete information, even when such information could be acquired. The books they choose to read, for instance — and this surely comprises an important sector of their existence — they select not by reason of the real value of the book, but from what they have heard of its content. We are all obliged, by lack of time, to act without complete information.

Two Tasks for Advertising

Advertising is another example of something we can understand better, if we allow for the time it takes to acquire information. We then see that advertising has two separate functions, since there are two different kinds of information to be disseminated. To begin with, advertising is a means of making factual knowledge more accessible than otherwise. Second, it serves to provide quasi information for people who lack the time to acquire the genuine insights. They get the surrogate information they want to have, in order to feel that they are making the right decision. The people responsible for advertising thus make use of the recipient's information costs on two planes. First, they gain an effect by cutting down the recipient's information costs. Secondly, they exploit his propensity to accept persuasion, when he is unwilling to devote time to collecting sufficient information for independent action. The advertiser helps to close the information gap, at the same time exploiting the information gap that is bound to remain.

Obviously, there is no clear boundary between these two types of advertising. One and the same advertisement can fulfill the two purposes. The time situation of the recipient will determine the emphasis. If he is prepared to obtain very detailed information, then the advertising will be informative in character. This applies, for instance, to the advertising directed to firms, which have after all much greater resources than households to effect a thorough investigation before procurement. If, on the other hand, the recipient is not prepared to obtain detailed information, then the advertisements aimed at him will be more in the nature of information surrogates.

As the scarcity of time increases, the emphasis in advertising will be displaced in the direction of ersatz information. The object will be to provide a motive for an action for which no solid argument exists. Those, like George Katona, who believe that advertising will become increasingly informative are the victims of pious hopefulness. Instead, increasing reliance will be placed on "hidden persuaders," which are what the consumers need to be able to make a quick decision. Venus and Mars will play an ever-increasing role in advertising. Brand loyalty must be built up among people who have no possibility of deciding how to act on objective grounds. As routine purchasing procedures gain in importance as a means of reducing decision-making time, it will become increasingly important to capture those who have not yet developed their routines.

There has been, as we know, an enormous increase in the volume of advertising. Since 1945, the *Printers' Ink* advertising index has risen by 400 per cent. During the corresponding 20-year period, Gross National Product and private consumption in the United States only doubled. This is what we should expect as the result of the declining quality of decisions. As the need for an information surrogate grows, it is increasingly necessary for the individual manufacturer to keep up with the rest in influencing easily influenced purchasers.

It is doubtful how far this development can continue. It is true that as the level of incomes continues to rise, the quality of decision-making will fall still further and increase the free play for influence. We must not forget, however, that as the volume of advertising increases, the effect of each individual message is bound to decline. Obviously, different messages are competing with each other for the recipient's time. Advertisers have reportedly begun to devote increased attention to this fact. They are aware that a growing number of messages never succeed in reaching the consumers. In newspapers packed with advertising, people will for reasons of time act in such a way as not to be exposed to it all. To counteract this, advertising agencies are assigning increased importance to visual dominance, or to penetrating through to the consumer in other ways. The prime object is actually to reach the recipient who is acting under pressure of time. The existence of this problem is clear from calculations showing that the average American is exposed to sixteen hundred advertising messages per day, and that he is reached in the course of a year, via radio and television, by ten thousand commercials. Figures of this type are obviously dependent on how we decide to reckon. But even if other methods might give different results, the figures show clearly enough what might ultimately limit the volume increase in advertising. Total expenditure on publicity, on the other hand, can go on rising still farther. As advertisers approach the upper volume limit, it is probable that they will accept higher and higher costs for each individual message, in order to increase its penetrative power.

This interpretation of the role of advertising, which stems from an increasing scarcity of time, differs considerably from the views usually encountered. There are two schools. The critics suggest that consumers are irrational and that malevolent marketers are manipulating them. Advertising is a cause of — and not the result of — a declining quality of decisions. Advertising is considered to grow in scale as we move away from our basic wants, and the free play for manipulation increases. The defenders of advertising claim that the consumers are rational and that they cannot therefore be influenced to make dim-witted purchases. Advertising simply helps them to avoid mistakes in their purchasing.

Both these views are dubious. People can be made the victims of persuasion, not because they are irrational, but because they are rational. Since they are rational, they are not prepared to spend all their time gathering information on what are the best things to buy. The increase in the volume of advertising can hardly be attributed to sales departments having become increasingly malevolent, or the customers increasingly irrational. In both these respects, human nature is surely neither better nor worse than it has always been. Nor can the distance from basic wants play any independent role. There is no reason to suppose that we reflect more carefully about what shoes to buy than what skates.

The critics of advertising exhort people to be intelligent customers. Insofar as the quality of purchasing decisions falls below its optimal level, such exhortations are justified. It is probable, however, that they are often out of place. Only if one possesses complete information can one behave in a way that the critics would judge to be intelligent. But to obtain complete information, one would have in fact to function very unintelligently. One would spend all one's time reading consumer reports, and otherwise acquiring information on economic matters. The majority of people will find, on calculation or reflection, that this would be an uneconomic way of allocating their time. That a person may buy more consumer reports as his income rises — as might be expected when such reports become relatively cheaper — does not mean that he necessarily reads them more. And even if the total time devoted to consulting such reports rises, it would not imply more study being given to them per decision. By accepting a number of mistakes, one will gain more than sufficient

time to offset these mistakes by greater income from work. But as
soon as one lacks complete information, one is also exposed to the
possibility of being influenced by advertising. One actually *wants* to be
influenced by advertising to get an instant feeling that one has a perfectly good reason to buy this or that commodity, the true properties
of which one knows dismally little about. Only unintelligent buyers
acquire complete information.

"The backward art of spending money"

Even if the time for reflection per decision is reduced, the total
time spent in acquiring information can increase. If the total number
of decisions increases more quickly than the time per decision falls,
then there will be an increase in the total time devoted to gathering
information. What happens in practice will depend on how the yield
on decision-making time alters as time per decision is reduced. The
yield must be brought into parity with what it is in other sectors of
use, and the question will be how much the time per decision must
be cut until this equilibrium is reached. If it has to be greatly reduced, then the total amount of time spent on decision-making will
fall, and vice versa. One can perhaps hazard a guess that total decision-making time has increased, parallel with a decline in quality of
decisions owing to a shorter time per decision. In this case we have
a decline of decision-making in a decision-making economy, just as
on the general level we have a decline of service in the service
economy.

Total decision-making time will depend also on how the difficulty
of decision-making changes, as economic growth faces the consumers
with new decisions. If decisions become more difficult, then the yield
on decision-making time will increase. We should then have a tendency for total decision-making time also to increase. There are many
grounds for supposing that the products on which decisions must be
made are in practice becoming increasingly complicated. Even good
honest food is now not as easy to appraise as we might think. As
Dexter Masters points out: "We no longer have many really simple

products: fresh fluid milk is a manufactured article; ham is adulterated with water; meat is tenderized with enzymes; bread is processed and chemicalized; fruits and vegetables are injected with dyes and coated with waxes; poultry is dosed with hormonal drugs."

But the most interesting thing, from all aspects, is not total decision-making time, but the time spent per decision. W. C. Mitchell, over fifty years ago, wrote a famous paper on "the backward art of spending money." He pointed out the great differences prevailing between the quality of the decisions made where money is earned, i.e., in production, and the decisions made where it is spent, i.e., in consumption. The reason for this is not any essential difference in the nature of production and consumption. As we have already repeatedly emphasized, the activities of the household are a form of production. That this is true of personal work is obvious. But even when we devote ourselves to the enjoyment of consumer goods, we are engaged in the production of a material utility or satisfaction — the end product of the economic process. No one has clarified the similarities between consumption and production in a more entertaining manner than A. K. Cairncross, who points out that a household contains all the functions of which a company is built. There is a procurement department and a sales department. The latter normally sells labor. There is a transport department, which handles above all the transport of children between different activities. Households are afflicted by labor problems, and wage negotiations. Unwilling children can actually go on strike to improve their benefits. The list of parallels could be extended.

But if we consider the household as a productive unit, we understand also why the declining quality of decisions that we have discussed is bound to occur. The households are small productive units, in which there is very little space for productivity improvements in decision-making. At the same time, real wage increases are taking place in production. This means that the requirement for yield on other time increases. But the yield on time spent in gathering information can be raised only by reducing this amount of time per decision, acquiring only the most important information. But by cutting down the collection of information in this way, we reduce the quality of our decisions. If W. C. Mitchell were able to rewrite his essay today, he would probably find cause to employ much stronger words than he did fifty years ago.

What has been said above, however, does not imply that we are becoming increasingly irresponsible when it comes to adjusting total expenditure to our existing income. People cut their coats according to their cloth, as much as they ever did. The advantages of making the right decision on this point will grow as our incomes rise, which means that the costs of making the right decision will not undergo a relative increase. The quality of this special decision will, therefore, remain unchanged. But the average quality of the growing volume of decisions involved in our total expenditure will decline. This is one reason, among many, why real income is increasing more slowly than the statistics would suggest.

CHAPTER VII

The Acceleration of Consumption

A little prince was to make
an excursion; they asked him:
"Would Your Highness like to
ride a horse or sail in a boat?"
And he answered: "I want to ride
a horse and sail in a boat."

Hjalmar Söderberg

Consumption Time and the Allocation of Time

The time devoted to enjoying different consumption goods is as essential in the consumption process as the goods themselves. This is why it is not only possible, but actually necessary, to regard time as a scarce resource and to investigate how it is distributed over different fields of use. If we ignore the fact that consumption, like work and other activities, takes time, then we shall portray development, as economic theory still does, as if a rising level of incomes led to everyone getting more and more "free time" and to the relaxing of the general pace of life. It is, therefore, of basic importance to try to decide how changes in the average level of incomes will influence consumption time.

An Increasing "Goods Intensity"

It is difficult to decide a priori whether or not *total* consumption time will increase. This we observed when discussing changes in work time. Whether or not total consumption time changes, will depend on how easy it is to substitute goods for time in the consumption process. If it is easy, then an increase in productivity will entail our working more to increase the volume of consumption goods beyond what the increase would have been with unchanged working hours. If, on the other hand, it is difficult to substitute goods for time then there must be an increase in consumption time when the volume of goods increases as the result of rising productivity.

In a numerical example in the chapter on work time, the assumption was made that goods and time must be combined in fixed proportions in the consumption process. It was assumed to be impossible to substitute goods for time. In these circumstances, the total consumption time will increase (and work time decrease) when productivity rises. Fixed proportions between time and goods in consumption represent, however, an extreme case and an improbable one. When we conceive of a certain possibility of substituting goods and time, we can no longer decide a priori how far the total time devoted to consumption will change.

However, it is not only changes in total consumption time that are of interest. It is also of value to know something about how the consumption time per consumption item changes. If we assume fixed proportions between goods and time in consumption, this will obviously mean that the consumption time per product is constant. This assumption, as we said, represents a special case. Insofar as it is possible to substitute goods for time, we probably do so. The time spent per item will in all likelihood decline. This is because goods are becoming cheaper in relation to time, and it will then pay to use more goods in relation to time. To increase their material welfare, people will thus make their consumption time more "commodity intensive." Against this background, we can also observe that work time, following a productivity increase, is most unlikely to be so reduced that the increase in total consumption time will be greater than the increase in the volume of goods. If it were, the goods intensity in consumption would decline.

By an increase in goods intensity we push up the yield per time unit in consumption. The more goods we consume per time unit, the greater the yield on the margin on the time devoted to consumption. This is an economic principle in line, for instance, with the notion that the more equipment a worker has at his disposal, the greater the yield on each working hour. This increase in the yield per time unit in consumption is also what is needed for an equilibrium to prevail. The yield per time unit has risen in production, and equilibrium requires that the yield on time be equally high in all activities. For the same reason, we have already noted that the yield per time unit in maintenance work must be raised — and in various ways will be raised. The forces working for a shorter maintenance time per product, however, are still stronger than those working for a shorter consumption time per item.

The acceleration of consumption, which means that increasingly little time will be devoted to each consumption item, can take various forms. A more expensive version of a commodity, for instance, can be used for the same time as was previously devoted to a less expensive type; a man, say, buys a Morris Major instead of a Morris Minor when his income rises. Or he may exchange his black telephone for a colored one. Another way in which consumption can accelerate is by what we can call "simultaneous consumption," when a consumer tries to enjoy more than one consumption product at the same time. He may keep his Morris Minor, but install a television set in it. Or, after dinner, he may find himself drinking Brazilian coffee, smoking a Dutch cigar, sipping a French cognac, reading *The New York Times,* listening to a Brandenburg Concerto and entertaining his Swedish wife — all at the same time, with varying degrees of success. A third method of accelerating consumption is what we may term "successive consumption." One enjoys one commodity at a time, but each one for a shorter period. Instead of spending two hours driving for pleasure, one may drive for an hour and devote the other hour to sailing — a pleasure that one could not afford with one's previous level of income. The degree of utilization of the capital stock represented by consumption goods will then decline.

In actual fact the differences between these three forms of acceleration are not very marked. A larger car, for instance, can be regarded, if we like, as a form of simultaneous consumption: its size gives further dimensions to the pleasure of having a car, conferring prestige, if not increased mobility. In the same way, the differences between simultaneous and successive consumption are often small. It can be difficult to decide, for instance, whether the person eating in front of the television is simultaneously eating and viewing, or whether he is alternating between the one and the other. But even if it is difficult in practice to draw any clear boundaries, it can be interesting to keep them apart conceptually. To illustrate both the similarity and the difference, we can say that in simultaneous consumption there are more consumption activities per time unit, while in successive consumption there is less time per commodity unit.

Waxing and Waning Pleasures

We have noted that it is difficult to decide a priori how total consumption time will change when productivity increases. We have established, on the other hand, that the goods intensity of consumption is likely to increase, i.e., that the proportion of goods to time in consumption will rise. A third question which remains to be discussed is how the time devoted to different consumption activities will alter in relation to total consumption time. There will probably occur certain reallocations of time within total consumption time. Charting the principles these will follow may give some valuable insights into our changing existence.

The reason for a reallocation of time among different activities is that an increase in the goods intensity will increase the yield on time to different degrees in different activities. The pleasure derived from the time spent on certain activities will hardly increase at all if we try to increase the goods intensity. In other activities, however, an increase in the goods intensity will give a marked increase in the yield on time. To achieve an equilibrium, it is necessary that the yield on time on the margin be equally high in all activities. Higher productivity and a greater volume of goods will, therefore, mean that the proportion of total consumption time devoted to certain activities will rise, while that devoted to others will accordingly decrease. If total consumption time is constant, there will thus be a decline in absolute figures in the time devoted to activities that are not particularly dependent on goods.

Let us assume that we have only two consumption activities, one of which demands a minimum of goods for its perfect exercise, while the other is highly dependent on the number of goods with which the time spent on it can be combined. When the level of productivity rises and the volume of goods increases, the yield on time spent in activity number 2 will increase, while the yield on time in activity number 1 will remain constant. Obviously, one can profit — providing one's taste for the two activities remains unchanged — from displacing time from the first to the second activity. This reallocation of time will continue to a point at which the time spent on both pleasures gives on the margin an equally high yield.

This reallocation of time is important. Many activities are by nature such as to be highly dependent on the volume of consumption goods that can be made available. Many other pleasures — ancient and venerable — are such that their intensity cannot be heightened by using more goods during the time in which they are practiced. These activities will be subject to increasingly tough competition for time and will run the risk of taking an increasingly inferior place.

The Income Elasticity of Activities

All these different arguments can be summed up to advantage with the help of the concept of "income elasticity." By income elasticity, economists usually mean the way in which the demand for goods changes in relation to changes in income. If the level of income rises, it is probable that the demand for goods will increase. Its income elasticity is then said to be positive. If the demand increases more rapidly than income, then its income elasticity is higher than 1. In the event that demand should fall when incomes rise, then the goods in question have a negative income elasticity. They are "inferior goods." If the fraction of income saved remains constant, then total demand has an income elasticity of 1. This means that a weighted average of the income elasticity of different goods, with a constant ratio of saving, is also 1. If we consider how the income elasticity of a given item alters with successive increases in income, we will probably find high values when the item is something new. Gradually, demand will no longer rise more quickly than income. At at even later stage, when the item encounters increased competition from new products, the income elasticity will fall below 1 and may actually become negative.

In the same way, we can speak of the income elasticity of an activity. There we relate, on the one hand, a change in the amount of time allocated to a certain pursuit and, on the other, a change in level of income. If more time is devoted to the pursuit in question when incomes rise, then it will be said to have a positive income elasticity. If the percentage increase in time is greater than that of income, then the income elasticity will be above 1. If the time spent on it declines, then we have an "inferior pursuit."

The fact that we cannot state a priori whether or not the time devoted to consumption purposes will increase when incomes rise means that we cannot decide in advance whether this activity has a positive or negative income elasticity. That consumption will be increasingly commodity intensive, means that consumption goods have a higher income elasticity than does consumption time. Since total consumption has an income elasticity amounting to a value of 1, we can draw the conclusion that consumption time can have a maximum income elasticity of 1. We also know that the total time at the disposal of the individual is constant. This means that the weighted average income elasticity of all activities — not only consumption activities — is zero. If consumption time is constant, then we also know that the average income elasticity of consumption activities is zero. It is interesting to compare this with the average elasticity of goods, which amounts to 1.

We have also established that the time allocated to different activities will alter, for the reason that different pursuits are variously suited to enhancement by an increase in the goods intensity. Since the average income elasticity of activities will amount approximately to a value of zero, we can therefore draw the conclusion that many consumption activities will be inferior, i.e., that the time devoted to them will decline as incomes rise.

Against this background, we can study various examples of consumption activities. We will expect to reach different conclusions from those usually drawn. It is typical to imagine that one does more of everything as one's income rises. One may possibly *buy* more of everything, but one cannot conceivably *do* more of everything. The income elasticity of goods is usually confused with the income elasticity of time. The purchase of more expensive golf clubs is taken as an indication that golfers are devoting themselves more to their sport.

The Declining Pleasures of the Table . . .

Just as the goods that have long been available on the market are probably the first to have to move over when new products are launched, so too is it probable that the activities to which increasingly little time will be devoted are the traditional pleasures. These include eating. When discussing the need to reduce maintenance time, we were able to observe that the pleasures of the table are under pressure, and we encounter now a further reason why this should be the case. Since there is a limit — for most people a fairly low one — to how far the pleasures of sitting at table can be enhanced by increasing the amount and quality of the food, it is probable that eating will become an inferior pursuit. In this way much of the pleasure of eating is eliminated. A primary pleasure with deep psychological dimensions is reduced to a maintenance function. The time spent in acquiring the necessary number of calories and vitamins must often be improved by reading the newspaper or looking at television.

. . . and of the Bed

Another ancient and well-established pleasure is physical love — if this circumspect, clinical term can be accepted by those who would prefer a lustier expression. In view of the enormous amount of "sex" that is believed to characterize our age, it is perhaps somewhat provocative to suggest that we are devoting less and less time to it. However, there are very good grounds for such an assertion.

To treat sexual matters in a work on economics is no innovation. Economists have discussed sex as a conceivable obstacle to economic growth, while I shall be discussing economic growth as a conceivable obstacle to sex. Even since the time of Malthus, a certain aversion to sex has been noticeable in the economic literature, since it is practices of this kind that give rise to the enormous problem of overpopulation. The development of contraceptive methods, however, has made it possible for economists and others to worry about population problems without having to accept Malthus' "positive controls." Economists, if asked, would probably say that economic growth has had a stimulating effect on sexual activities. High levels of education, a result of economic growth, have eliminated much superstition and permitted a freer flow of emotions. Also, thanks to economic growth, contraceptives have become not only technically but also financially available.

Such arguments are probably correct enough in themselves. Certain forces, however, are acting in the contrary direction. Love takes time. To court and love someone in a satisfactory manner is a game with many and time-consuming phases. To illustrate how economic growth affects the allocation of time to love, we can observe that the pleasure achieved by an embrace can hardly be intensified by increasing the number of goods consumed during the period in question. Goods in fact would only be in the way, beyond the minimum requirement in respect of furniture. In this respect love differs from most other activities, and it is this that has made its status so vulnerable. A moralist may be glad to learn that love has a negative income elasticity. It is an "inferior" activity — although inferior in another sense than that employed by the moralist.

One can distinguish three different ways in which efforts to save time in our love life manifest themselves. Affairs, which by their very nature occupy a great deal of time, become less attractive; the time spent on each occasion of love-making is being reduced; the total number of sexual encounters is declining.

To keep a mistress is an institution requiring considerable time.

Disraeli devoted much attention — perhaps mainly of a Platonic nature — to Lady Chesterfield, at times when our non-Victorian Prime Ministers and Presidents address themselves energetically to hard work. People in exalted — and even less exalted — offices should now, it is thought, be on the job from morning to night. The mistress, as an institution, is disappearing. Who has time these days for intimate lunches in conversation with an attractive woman? The French institution of the *cinq-à-sept* — two hours for which love-seeking husbands do not always feel bound to account — is reported to be disappearing in the increased hustle of life even in France. On the whole, it is probable that conjugal fidelity is increasing, if not in thought, at least in practice. It takes too much time to establish new contacts, as compared with relaxation in the home. For the same reason, perhaps, young and energetic people tend to marry early and cut down on the time-consuming process of search.

Of course, new sexual contacts are still being established, and on a large scale, particularly among the unmarried. The increasing scarcity of time should in this case lead to these contacts being after increasingly brief preliminary approaches. Since there is no time for repeated lunches, during which one reconnoiters the lay of the land, one has to show one's inclinations more directly. Modern love affairs are reminiscent, according to Sebastian de Grazia, of business agreements: "No frills, new flowers, no time wasted in elaborate compliments, verses, and lengthy seductions, no complications, and no scenes, please." Such a system is designed to save time, and it presupposes what we mean by "sexual freedom." Those who complain that girls these days are "easy" fail to understand that in a hectic age girls must accelerate to save time, both for themselves and for their male friends. It would be inconceivable, for reasons of time, that a modern young lady should require her presumptive lover — as she did in a Noh play I once had the pleasure of seeing — to appear for one hundred evenings and wait outside her door, to be admitted on the hundred-and-first. The smooth character parodied in the well-known film *The Knack* is described as requiring only "two minutes from start to finish." This is much more typical behavior in an age with an increasing scarcity of time.

Modern people do not only try to save time in the actual establish-
ment of contact. The man in *The Knack* obviously saved time on every
lap of the course. It is only to be expected that people who are in a
hurry should become the devotees of instant love. The ultimate way
of saving time, of course, is to refrain entirely from this pleasure, or
at least to such degree as may be possible without disrupting psychological effects. Such a method is obviously not alien to people today.
As a by-product of a sociological study of some eighty-three hundred
business executives, W. Lloyd Warner and James C. Abegglen were
able to make a number of interesting observations on the situation of
their wives. We learn, for instance, that the wife of an executive
"must not demand too much of her husband's time or interest. Because of his single-minded concentration on the job, even his sexual
activity is relegated to a secondary place."

Even individuals belonging to less harried classes seem to save
time in the same way. It may surprise some readers to learn that,
according to an article in *Gaudeamus* — the Stockholm University
student newspaper — female students are complaining that their male
colleagues fail to take time off for love. They are so engrossed in
their studies. The female students — and how, by the way, do they
come to have more time? — are obliged to turn to foreign students or
"ordinary" young men.*

When we leave the executive world and student life, we can still
find signs that love is suffering from the competition of other activities. It is well known that the big blackout in New York in November 1965 was followed, nine months later, by a spectacular rise in the
birth-rate. With nothing else to do, people did what could be done in
the dark. *Faute de mieux on couche avec sa femme,* in a modern
version. Some may have groped their way from the television set to
the bed to seek support in what must have been a moment of fear.
A boring lack of alternatives, however, must surely have played its
part. This at any rate would seem to explain why the birth rate in

---

* The Latinist may enjoy the contradiction between the name of the newspaper and the message conveyed. As one may guess, the name is the relic of
a less harried age.

Chicago rose by 30 per cent nine months after the worst snowstorm in memory (in January 1967). In underdeveloped countries, the birth rate reportedly falls in villages when electricity is installed. The pleasures of the night suffer competition from the extended day. To add to our list of empirical guesses, we may perhaps suggest that the phenomenon of shipboard romances is due simply to the abnormal amount of time available.

In various ways, the increasing scarcity of time can thus divert time from Venus. Only insofar as our Victorian inhibitions have been dissipated and love is now in favor is there any force to offset the effects of the time scarcity. This counterforce is probably not sufficient to have created any movement in the direction of more love, particularly since there also exist changes in taste which have thinned our desires. The reason for this is that a decreasing amount of time for love reduces its attractions. As Ovid writes in "The Remedies for Love":

> *Tam Venus otia amat;*
> *qui finem quaeris amoris,*
> *Credit amor rebus;*
> *res age, tutus eris.* *

In reading these lines, one should remember that Ovid surely means that not only work, but also other consumption activities, will have a negative influence on the passions. To quote another representative of the arts, Charles Baudelaire: *Il est malheureusement bien vrai que, sans le loisir . . . l'amour ne peut être qu'une orgie de roturier que l'accomplissement d'un devoir conjugal. Au lieu du caprice brûlant ou revêur, il devient une répugnante utilité.*†

Ovid and Baudelaire alike published their warnings in an age when a scarcity of time was the exception. Now that it is the rule, their assessment of the conditions necessary to love are even more worthy

---

* "So does Venus delight in leisure;
 you who seek an end of love,
 love yields to busyness;
 be busy and you will be safe."
 † "It is sad but only too true that without . . . the leisure, love is incapable of rising above a grocer's orgy or the accomplishment of a conjugal duty. Instead of being a passionate or poetic caprice, it becomes a repulsive utility."

of consideration. For those who find poets unreliable, we can quote other authorities in evidence that a quickening pace of life deadens the emotions. Anyone who cares to study a sexual manual will find that great emphasis is placed on the ruinous effects of chronological shortcuts. Yet perhaps the writers of these books, as members of the harried leisure class, have also fallen victim to the cooling effects of the time scarcity on appetite. David Riesman in *The Lonely Crowd* makes the following observation: "The older marriage manuals, such as that of Van der Velde (still popular, however), breathe an ecstatic tone, they are travelogues of the joy of love. The newer ones, including some high school sex manuals, are matter of fact, toneless, and hygienic — Boston Cooking School style."

"Sex is Dead" proclaimed a well-written and amusing article in the *Christian Century* in 1966, presenting a variety of evidence that the taste for love has declined. Obviously, this obituary does not mean, any more than does our argument of the increasing scarcity of time, that physical love has been entirely eliminated. People have not stopped making love, any more than they have stopped eating. But — to extend the surprisingly adequate parallel with the joys of gastronomy — less time is devoted to both preparation and savoring. As a result, we get an increasing amount of frozen nutrition at rapid sittings — the time, on occasion, being too short for any effort to be made at all at stilling the hunger. A pleasure has been turned into the satisfaction of a basic need — "a grocer's orgy" — a maintenance function — a conjugal duty.

Interestingly enough, such a status of love is in itself compatible with the doctrines voiced by certain schools of thought within the Christian Church: physical love is required for the multiplication of souls, and as such it is therefore acceptable as long as it is quick, not particularly frequent, and always within the family. In this lies a perfect irony. Just as medieval regulations in the economic sector were abolished to permit the Industrial Revolution, so have various inhibiting rules in the social and ethical sector been crushed by an age inspired by the philosophy of pleasure. Yet the supposedly amoral members of this irreligious age have found no cause to avail themselves of their erotic freedom, and they behave in practice more in conformity with the previous moral laws than those who originally formulated them.

Even if all this is worth saying and may seem plausible enough, are there not clear signs to the contrary? Has not our age actually been called oversexed? The phenomena, however, that have led to this epithet do not conflict with the idea that economic growth has led to certain efforts to save time in the erotic sector. Let us consider in more detail three phenomena which are customarily taken as a sure sign that modern people are a lusty lot. The first is that sexual contacts are being made at an increasingly early age. What this implies is simply that young people, who have not yet achieved the income level of the harried leisure class, have exploited the freedoms originally created with a view to adult welfare. Another sign often quoted is that sexual unions are becoming casual, i.e., the result of increasingly short acquaintanceship. The fact, however, that people take less time is rather an indication that they spend less time on loving. They are in a hurry, and so each contact must proceed faster. Thirdly, all pornography is taken as evidence of great sexual activity. This, however, may be a case of smoke without fire. Pinups and other manifestations of quasi sex serve to give satisfaction from looking, rather than from doing. A love life consisting of a series of extremely quick encounters tends to be frustrating. In this situation, a few lively films can function as a rapid and convenient manner of experiencing certain sensations. The change in female ideals is probably indicative of modern ways of life. The mystique of a Marlene Dietrich has little to give a generation that is not interested in doing it and doing it well. Contemporary sex queens are more conducive to satisfaction from just looking, or possibly hoping for a quick "touch-and-go."

Some Waxing Pleasures

There are some types of consumption to which an increasing amount of time is allocated. This group contains the pleasures that can fairly easily be increased in intensity by raising the volume of goods per time unit.

People have a surprising liking for large banquets, conventions and cocktail parties. One explanation for this may be that it seems a highly efficient way of exploiting the time allocated to social intercourse. One meets a lot of people at once. One devotes oneself to the simultaneous consumption of food and people. To be the only guests to dinner is normally considered less flattering than to be invited with many others. In a way, it should be the other way round. Perhaps it is not flattering because it suggests that your time is at such a low price that you are content to meet a couple of people at a time. Efforts to economize one's time in this way lead in due course to one's having numerous acquaintances and no friends.*

The clearest examples of pleasure that are on the increase will be found among activities based on the use of things. The average income elasticity of such pursuits will be high. The environment of the typical consumer is a dense jungle of things: a house and a summer cottage; cars and a boat; TV, radio, and a record player; records, books, newspapers, and magazines; clothes and sports clothes; tennis racket, badminton racket, squash racket, and table tennis racket; footballs, beach balls, and golf balls; basement, attic, and closets, and all they contain. It is the total time spent in using all these things that increases; simultaneously, however, the time allocated to each of them individually is declining.

If we divide the various activities in this group into different components, we will naturally find that all these different activities are not claiming more time. They are mutually competing for time, and so many things, though still usable, will actually not be used at all. Many people will have a tennis racket lying somewhere and never used, or a croquet set left idle in some corner. Even if economic theory appears to teach us that goods afford utility, regardless of the time devoted to them, these objects will still be experienced by the individual as valueless. If their owner can find time to throw them away — the ultimate maintenance function — then they will be thrown. In this way, accelerating consumption leads to a throw-away system, owing to the lack of consumption time. A defense put for-

* The same effect is produced by another way of saving time to which people sometimes resort: the circularized Christmas letter.

ward against accusations that firms sell products with built-in ob-
solescence (i.e., with a shorter lifetime than they could have, without
extra cost in manufacture) is that people do not want to have their
possessions for so long and that one might as well allow for this in
production.

One particular pursuit has come to play a major role in the efforts
of individuals to raise the goods intensity of their consumption. This
is photography. A tourist, for instance, need no longer content himself with enjoying what he sees. He can give himself a feeling of really
using his time by taking pictures. Cameras have made it possible to
raise the goods intensity of many pursuits. It is easy to understand
why love is so vulnerable to competition, if we reflect that we are
spending time on only one person and cannot even take photographs
of the occasion.

The Risks of Acceleration

Consumption is being accelerated to increase the yield on time devoted to consumption. There is naturally a risk that an increased
goods intensity and the allied reallocation of time will in fact lead to
the opposite result, or at least not provide optimum satisfaction. We
know that wealth is no guarantee of happiness. To try to explain why
this is the case would be presumptuous and would lead far from the
main theme of this essay. Even so, it may be of some interest to point
out that rising incomes can lead to a declining yield on consumption
time.

Walter Kerr, in his fascinating book *The Decline of Pleasure,* has
claimed that the present requirement that time should be used to give
a high yield prevents relaxed enjoyment. This may well be so. The
activities crowded onto the belt unrolled by time can encroach upon
each other. As an example of a dubiously pleasurable form of simultaneous consumption, we can quote the following from Kerr's book:

> We have had Music to Read by, Music to Make Love By, Music to
> Sleep By, and, as one humorist has had it, Music to Listen to Music By.
> What is interesting about these titles is that they so candidly describe the

position of the popular arts in our time. They admit at the outset that no one is expected to sit down, for heaven's sake, and attend to the music. It is understood that, while the music is playing, everyone within earshot is going to be busy doing something else . . .

To take another example of dubious simultaneous consumption, the constant amateur photographer may lose his ability to appreciate the moment. Such a person is pawning the present for an uncertain future. Particularly in those activities which, to be enjoyable, require excellence, discipline, and patience, efforts to save time can prove fatal. Such pursuits become uninteresting, if not an actual torture. Cultivation of the mind, at any serious level, belongs to this category. To quote Erich Fromm: ". . . anyone who ever tried to master an art knows that patience is necessary if you want to achieve anything. If one is after quick results, one never learns an art. Yet, for modern man, patience is as difficult to practice as discipline and concentration. Our whole industrial system fosters exactly the opposite: quickness."

If the increasing scarcity of time corrupts the pleasure of cultivating our minds, then this will be a serious consequence, and it is a problem that we shall be considering in a separate chapter.

The risks to which Kerr and Fromm have drawn attention involve the consumer who is *unconsciously* deviating from an optimal allocation of time. There is another danger, namely, that we will often *consciously* depart from the time allocation we would really like to follow. This is the result of a tendency to overmortgage our assets of time and of the fact that consumption time is the kind most easily reduced in a tight situation. Many people underestimate the maintenance requirements of different goods. When these requirements make themselves felt, consumption time is used as a buffer. Anyone who has acquired a swimming pool may have been unhappily surprised to find himself obliged to devote so much time to maintaining it that he is unable to swim in it. It is easy to find examples of a maintenance blindness, which disrupts people's plans for their time. There is also a sort of pleasure blindness. Many people have surely made the mistake of acquiring different articles, without reflecting that it takes time to use them. People with incomes that will soon be more typical may have joined both a golf club and a sailing club, only to discover that they lack the time really to utilize the privileges of both. Or else to give the impression of using them and to soothe their consciences, they perhaps veer between both activities in a way that is surely incompatible with a leisured existence in any sense of the word. It is easy to ignore the fact that goods require both time to maintain and time to enjoy, and this form of blindness leads to a suboptimal allocation of time.

CHAPTER VIII

Culture Time

INTERVIEWER: Vous pensez aussi que le
roman classique est mort?
ALBERTO MORAVIA: Pas absolument . . . Mais le
monde moderne n'a plus le temps de lire.

A Goal of Economic Progress

The cultivation of the mind and spirit is generally accepted as being the supreme goal of human effort. These pursuits supposedly raise our civilization above anything our inferiors in the Darwinian chain can achieve. This is the attitude reflected in the Latin sentence: *Horas non numero nisi serenas* — only peaceful hours count.

The profane thinkers who developed the gospel of economic growth regarded economic progress as an active means of promoting cultural progress. They expected that more and more time would be devoted to cultivation of the spirit. In Tibor Scitovsky's words: "In short, they hoped that progress would turn more and more people into philosophers in their own image, engaged in the leisurely and philosophical contemplation of the world and its wonders." Much of the optimism of the Enlightenment thinkers was bound up with such expectations. Now that economics has developed into a science, its practitioners have lost interest in the ultimate purposes of economic growth and how far they can be achieved. Nor have the analytic tools developed been able to provide any insight into the interplay between economics and culture. A time allocation theory, however, can provide some guidance in this respect. It reveals what many might call a disturbing circumstance: economic growth subjects culture time to an increasing competition, and the time devoted to cultural exercises is probably decreasing.

Culture — an "Inferior Activity"

Most of those who have bothered to reflect on the matter at all probably live in the belief that economic growth, which increases our resources, is also bound to entail more resources being allocated to cultural ends and more time accordingly being devoted to cultivation of the mind and spirit. This argument, however, is extremely superficial.

As we have already observed, a certain reallocation of time will occur among different consumption activities. More time will be given over to activities in which an increased input of consumption goods contributes markedly to the total satisfaction. The pleasure derived from time spent in developing the mind and spirit is in fact very little dependent on goods. For this reason, such pursuits will be most attractive when the general level of income is low — although above that of a paralyzing poverty. As the average level of incomes continues to rise, new possibilities open up. Activities that are enhanced by a high goods intensity become increasingly attractive. Time will be reallocated in this direction. Only if there is a very strong successive increase in total consumption time can culture time also increase. Even if one might think that increased time would be needed in which to relax *from* consumption, increasing time will in fact be devoted to relaxation *for* consumption.

Thus there is a great risk that culture is a pursuit with a negative income elasticity. The cultivation of mind and spirit is quite simply an inferior activity. Aldous Huxley has summarized people's optimistic economic expectations and has regretfully seen through them in the following ironic and far-sighted passage:

Different prophets may differ in their estimate of relative importance of the various activities which make up what is generally known as "the higher life"; but they all agree that the lives of our leisured posterity will be high. They will eagerly make themselves acquainted with "the best that has been thought or said" about everything; they will listen to concerts of the classiest music; they will practice the arts and handicrafts . . . they will study the sciences, philosophy, mathematics and meditate on the lovely mystery of the world in which they live.

In a word, these leisured masses of a future . . . will do all the things which our leisured classes of the present time so conspicuously fail to do.

Changes among Cultural Pursuits

Not all cultural pursuits will be hit equally hard by the increasing competition for time. This is because different cultural pursuits differ with respect to their potential enhancement by an increased goods intensity. To admire attractive cloud formations or to reflect on the world at large requires only the individual's time and no goods at all. To enjoy having beautiful pictures on one's walls, on the other hand, requires less of the individual's own time in relation to the possible input of money. An interesting intermediate category is provided by the performing arts. These require in more equal proportions the individual's own time, a time on the part of the artists, and various goods in the form of premises and fittings.

The first category of pursuit will suffer particularly from the competition for time. Goods will become increasingly cheap and time more expensive, but these pursuits offer no possibility of substituting time for goods. More goods will not increase the pleasure derived, but actually reduce it. The true and unspoiled pleasures of the romantics are disappearing. No one has time to take pleasure in an autumn leaf, but many take time to admire the message of an expensive television set. In the following poem Marya Mannes sings the praises of such vanishing pleasures:

> Lie down and listen to the crabgrass grow,
> The faucet leak, and learn to leave them so.
> Feel how the breezes play about your hair
> And sunlight settles on your breathing skin.
> What else can matter but the drifting glance
> On dragonfly or sudden shadow there
> Of swans aloft and the whiffle of their wings
> On air to other ponds? Nothing but this:
> To see, to wonder, to receive, to feel
> What lies in the circle of your singleness.
> Think idly of a woman or a verse

> Or bees or vapor trails or why the birds
> Are still at noon. Yourself, be still —
> There is no living when you're nagging time
> And stunting every second with your will.
> You work for this: to be the sovereign
> Of what you slave to have — not
> Slave.

In our enjoyment of the performing arts, there is undoubtedly great free play to increase the input of something other than one's own time. One can go to more lavish — and thus perhaps also better — performances to increase the yield on one's time. This may suggest that increasing efforts will be made to raise the quality of performances, and that people will devote more time to admiring and enjoying the results. This, however, may well be an overhasty conclusion. An increased goods intensity will be attractive when the price of goods is falling, compared with the price of time, i.e., what happens when the level of productivity rises. But productivity in the performing arts is not easily raised. Not much can be done to mechanize Rigoletto. An unrehearsed Swan Lake is not particularly swanlike. The playing of a Beethoven symphony requires a given number of man hours. Any attempt to reduce the size of the orchestra, to play more quickly, or to cut the number of rehearsals will be greeted not as improved productivity but as a reduction in quality.

For this reason there will not, in our enjoyment of the performing arts, be any relative reduction in all the costs outside the individual's own time. Production costs, and thus the price of tickets, will rise comparatively with the price of goods, as does the cost of the individual's own time. Therefore, there will be no scope for a profitable increase in the intensity of nontime inputs in enjoyment of the performing arts. At most, one can try to increase the yield on time by more props on stage and the consumption of Dry Martinis in the interval. The competition for people's time will thus make itself felt in these arts. Only when an individual's income rises in relation to the average level will that part of the total costs that does not comprise his own time undergo a relative reduction.

There also exist, however, cultural pursuits in which it is undoubtedly possible to increase the goods intensity and thus the yield on time, when the prices of goods are falling in relation to the price of the individual's own time. As incomes rise, for instance, one can increase the pleasure of television viewing by procuring a more magnificent set. One can also, into the bargain, enjoy television performances of drama, ballet, and opera, which are available very cheaply on this medium. As incomes rise, one can also buy increasingly impressive high fidelity equipment and thus increase the pleasure of playing good music. By adding to one's record library, one can have the right music to hand for one's mood of the moment, and in this way increase the attractiveness of listening. In the same way, perhaps, one can enhance one's appetite for reading by keeping a private library and one's interest in art by building up a private collection. Rich people, for reasons of time economy, are collectors of art and not connoisseurs of ballet.

Even with these activities, however, the free play for such adjustments is probably fairly limited, compared with the situation in regular consumption activities. It is probably easier to enhance one's interest in sailing by increasing the size of one's sailboat than it is to enhance one's interest in reading by adding to one's library. Often, too, people probably buy art gadgets, like advanced high fidelity equipment, more from a technological interest than from any artistic appreciation, in this case, of improved sound reproduction. Insofar as the possibilities of raising the artistic yield by increased goods intensity are relatively limited, these cultural pursuits will also suffer from the pressure of time.

Changes in Taste

Parallel with economic growth, various changes in taste can occur and influence the allocation of time. It is possible, for instance, that the desire to pursue culture is increasing and that this will wholly or partly offset the negative effect of the limited possibility of increasing the goods intensity in such pursuits. It is also possible that tastes are changing in the opposite direction and reinforcing the tendency to reallocate time away from cultural pursuits. In actual practice, it is probable that considerable shifts in taste occur. We can distinguish at least two important causes of such changes. The first, which is strongest in the initial stages, tends to increase the interest in culture time. The other is in the reverse direction.

Parallel with economic growth, there has been a great increase in education. This raising of the educational level must surely have had a positive influence on cultural interest. General education has eliminated illiteracy and thus created one necessary condition for many of the cultural pursuits. Higher education has probably exercised a favorable effect on the more sophisticated forms of cultural activity. W. J. Baumol and W. G. Bowen report that theatregoers, for instance, have on the average a very high education. In the United States only 2.5 per cent of the audience is comprised of "blue collar workers," although the latter answer for 60 per cent of the town population. Swedner has found the same to hold true in Sweden. This type of statistics offers no causal connection, but at least it does not exclude the possibility that education stimulates an interest in cultural pursuits. This can also be claimed without contradicting the idea previously presented that a rising level of income exercises a negative effect on the time devoted to cultural pursuits. To begin with, we must observe the difference between a rise in the average level of income and a rise in the income of certain persons compared with all the others. A cross-section analysis can give different results from a time series analysis. Secondly, it is obviously possible that the positive changes in taste, in fact, offset the negative income changes, and that the net result of a rise in income is to increase the time devoted to culture.

It is probable, however, that rising levels of education have their greatest effect in an introductory stage of economic growth. A great deal of the increased education provided in a more advanced economy caters to narrow occupational requirements. It is presumably favorable for economic growth that higher education should be provided in public relations, data programming, and the art of being an air hostess. In *The Organization Man,* William Whyte discusses the increasing importance assigned to "the practical curriculum." J. K. Galbraith, in *The Affluent Society,* develops the same theme. The effect of this type of education on cultural appetites, however, would seem to be negligible.

There is also a risk of individual preferences changing in a direction which is likely to reduce the interest in culture. The increasing scarcity of time, which means an increasing tempo in both production and consumption, probably vitiates the pleasure of many cultural pursuits. (Harald Swedner, in an interview study from Sweden, reports that 40 per cent of those asked gave tiredness in the evenings as a reason for not attending the theatre as often as they might wish.) The time devoted to culture would in this case decline not only because it is difficult to increase the intensity of goods in this field, but also because the cultural appetite as such is declining. Concluding his analysis of the prerequisites for artistic pursuits, Erich Fromm is skeptical of the influence of modern conditions of life. We have already, as an introduction to the present argument, quoted Fromm's observation that the practice of an art demands great patience, while our entire system encourages the reverse quality of speed. Fromm also cites other requirements, such as discipline, concentration, and "supreme concern." Even if his requirements may seem severe when applied to the average earner's modest attempts at self-development, it is still possible to consider how well his requirements are met under different conditions. The conclusions reached by Fromm would seem compatible with what has already been said:

> Yet, even more than self-discipline, concentration is rare in our culture. On the contrary, our culture leads to an unconcentrated and diffused mode of life, hardly paralleled anywhere else. You do many things at once; you read, listen to the radio, talk, smoke, eat, drink. You are the consumer with the open mouth, eager and ready to swallow everything . . .

In a study designed to reveal the deep-going changes and differences between the patterns of life of different generations, Walter Kerr makes some similar observations:

> Neither my own children nor the children they bring home with them make any such commitments . . . (as the author made at an earlier age) . . . They seem content with a sampling of fragments: a fast flash of

horses racing into a gully toward a rendezvous they may not be around for, a man walking into a district attorney's office to report a crime they may or may not wish to hear solved, one-sixth of a wrestling match, the irising-out of an animated cartoon, the first roar of a cataract that would have ended as a commercial — a clattering continuum that need never become a continuity.

The mental energy and internal concentration required to cultivate the mind and spirit adequately are not easily mobilized after a hectic day. When one goes to a concert to relax after a busy day, the result can be a mild drowsiness — in itself pleasurable enough — rather than any spiritual uplift. It may be possible to arrive in a hurry at the kickoff at a football match without its ruining one's pleasure; but to have to rush to the overture at a theatre is to arrive in the wrong spirit.

The Controversy on Cultural Facts

There is a wide variety of views as to what effect economic growth has actually had on the cultural level and on the time devoted by individuals to the cultivation of mind and spirit. An enormous boom or a fatal degeneration; both judgments have been put forward. The interested reader may find the entire spectrum of opinions represented in the Spring 1960 issue of *Daedalus*. This lack of consensus is hardly surprising, in view of the inherently vague nature of all talk about "culture." All attempts at measurement are bound to fail. A person's observable behavior, for instance, can be misleading. This man may read, but to collect quotations rather than to deepen his understanding. That man may play Beethoven, but as a background to the evening's bridge. Another related complication is that a person can devote himself to something with a variety of intentions. A professor can experience intellectual pleasure in his discoveries, combined with pleasure in their potential implications for his career. *Two souls dwell, alas!, in my breast*, complains Faust. The culture discussions can also degenerate into a quarrel over quality. The "mass consumption of culture" is a description that has been used to evoke a feeling both of great achievement and of egregious degeneration.

The lack of consensus, however, is not the result merely of such difficulties in definition. Another reason for disagreement is the failure to specify the period of time over which comparisons are to be made. During the initial period of economic growth, it is probable that both rising incomes and rising levels of education have tended to increase the amount of time devoted to culture. Gradually, however, further increases in income, in combination with a more hectic way of living, have probably brought to bear a pressure on culture time, which has not been entirely offset by further increases in levels of education. If income increases and changes in taste have in this way had different effects at different periods, then our conclusions will depend on the periods we compare.

Even if there is a certain pressure on cultural time at present, it would be surprising if the total amount of time devoted to culture were not at a higher level than before the economic process began to pick up speed. This conclusion seems fair enough, even if we should not take it for granted that the situation in these respects was too miserable. In an apparently well-documented study on the standard of living in the United States in 1860, E. W. Martin shows a considerable level of cultural activity to have prevailed at the time.

[Chorus societies, amateur theaters and dramatic groups] often connected with literary and debating societies, were to be found in almost every community. Giving their performances in school buildings or small halls, with improvised costumes and properties, they — like the musical and literary organizations — provided an excuse for coming together and gave added interest to the lives of young people of village and country. In towns and cities they had more to work with, but they can hardly have given so much real enjoyment to participants and spectators.

But even if the scale of cultural pursuits has increased, it is indisputable that the upswing has failed to meet the hopes so long entertained. It is possible that the original cultural optimists entirely misjudged man's native character. It is also possible, however, that they ignored the fact that economic growth not only frees man from the requirement to work, but creates attractions other than spiritual cultivation, all of which compete for the time available. At any rate, no one nowadays will seriously claim that continued economic growth will lead to any marked cultural improvement. Only in the poorer countries dare people believe that economic progress will lead to cultural greatness. The program of the governing party in Mexico mentions the country's efforts to become a culturally great power, "which is and always has been the innermost aspiration of the Mexican people." In the wealthy countries, such optimism has given way to uncertainty. According to Sir Herbert Read: "There will [in the mid-eighties] be lights everywhere except in the mind of man, and the fall of the last civilization will not be heard above the incessant din."

The interesting question for the future is whether the rich countries are already in a phase in which cultural progress has not merely slowed down but actually given way to a decline, as expressed in people devoting increasingly less time the development of mind and spirit. Many would deny this, and are accustomed to quoting a wealth of statistics in support of their view. Many of these statistics, however, are easy to misinterpret. It is particularly important to guard against a deceptive use of figures on expenditure to suggest that we are experiencing a cultural boom. Such statistics have two shortcomings. To begin with, they can only show the scope of purchases of different items with cultural associations, and not the time devoted to their use. As we know, income increases mean that expenditure rises on the average more than consumption time. The income elasticity of the goods is greater than that of the activities. Statistics on expenditure are, therefore, a misleading indicator. That sales of pianos and records have gone up, need not mean that more time is necessarily being devoted to playing them. In the same way, the sale of books can increase steeply when incomes rise, without this proving that we read more.

The number of books published has increased considerably in recent decades. In the United States the number of new titles (including new editions) in 1950 was 11,000. By 1963, the figure was 19,000, and in 1964 it leapt to 28,500. We find the same picture if we investigate the number of books sold, the figures in the United States being 700 million in 1954 and 1,150 million by 1963. Even if one may question the merits of some of the books answering for this marked upswing, it is nonetheless impressive. As soon as we remember, however, that we are really interested not in how many books people buy, but how many they read, we experience some uncertainty. The relationship between books read and books purchased has in all probability changed, and it may well have changed so much as to mean that people read less now than they used to. If we multiply the number of books sold by an estimated average time for reading a book, we reach impossible figures. Many people must be in the habit of placing on their bookshelves works that they have bought but not read. When the books have lain on the bedside table for some length of time without being read, they are put out of the way, partly to stifle the voice of conscience and partly to provide space for more recently acquired books. The pleasure of buying books lies not so much in reading them as in having them available. People are buying books as they buy pictures — to glance at.

The use of expenditure statistics to throw light on the time devoted to cultural pursuits involves yet another risk. There will occur, as we know, a certain reallocation of time also within the time devoted to culture. The pursuits that will best hold their own are those geared to commodities. It is precisely these, however, which are covered by the figures on expenditure. Even if the expenditure statistic gave a fair picture of what is happening to the time devoted to these activities — which they do not — they would still give a distorted picture of the development of culture time as a whole. For the same reason, a measurement of what has happened to the time devoted to meditation, for instance, would give an excessively gloomy picture. The time spent in contemplation is probably approaching zero, without this meaning that culture time has yet been entirely eliminated.

In spite of these two difficulties, expenditure statistics are the source of information used by those wishing to claim that we have seen an impressive upturn in cultural interest. To give an example of the cavalier way in which even well-known research workers exploit such statistics to achieve their conclusions, we can quote from George Katona:

Americans buy gadgets instead of books — so it has been argued in envious Europe for many decades. Today Americans buy both gadgets and books. They have laborsaving devices which give them more free time to read books and attend lectures, go to concerts and theatrical performances, and visit museums. Sales of nonfiction paperback books showed a proportionately larger gain than the sales of most other products in the late 1950s and early 1960s, and the shares of book publishing companies have been considered growth stocks on the New York Stock Exchange. The more consumer goods people have, the more they spend on books, lectures, and concerts, as well as on schools and hospitals.

We are still far from a genuine mass culture. It is still a minority of families that spend more than a tiny portion of their income on educational and cultural needs. But the direction in which the society is moving is clear.

One type of expenditure data, however, does indicate correctly the time used by people in enjoyment of what they have bought, namely statistics on the purchase of tickets to performances in the scenic arts. People can very well be thought to buy books without reading them, but it would seem to be rare for people to buy such tickets without using them. Data are available in the United States in *Survey of Current Business*, "Admissions to Legitimate Theatre and Opera and Entertainments of Non-Profit Institutions (except athletics)." These have been quoted by adherents to the theory of a cultural boom. The Stanford Research Institute once pointed out in a report that consumers' expenditure on the arts increased during the period 1953–1960 by 130 per cent. This observation has since been frequently quoted and is considered very impressive, in that the increase is twice as great as that in expenditure on all types of recreation and more than six times higher than the increase for cinema tickets and tickets to sporting events.

W. J. Baumol and W. G. Bowen, in their excellent book on the economic dilemma of the performing arts, have subjected such figures to careful analysis. They found that in the period 1932–1963, ticket receipts from artistic performances increased by 8.3 per cent per year. During the period 1961–1963, the increase was only 4 per cent per year. As they point out, this is hardly a very spectacular increase. One must also remember that these figures had not been corrected for price and population increases. If we allow for price increases, the growth in total ticket receipts during the period 1929–1963 falls from 240 per cent to 65 per cent. If we then recalculate total ticket expenditure to expenditure per capita, the increase drops to 8 per cent for these three decades. "It is also interesting that, after falling sharply during the great depression, real expenditures per capita did not regain their 1929 level until 1960."

However, this criticism of data used to support the cultural boom doctrine should not be taken as suggesting that all cultural activities are at present declining. On the contrary. Changes in tastes can very well result in increased time being devoted to at least some activities. It is also, in fact, possible to find instances of cultural pursuits which seem to have expanded. Amateur activity in the arts in the United States, for instance, seems to be experiencing something of a boom. The number of symphony orchestras — mostly nonprofessional — in communities with fewer than 100,000 inhabitants has increased from some 600 in 1950 to over 1,000 in 1965. The same impression is gained from exploring how the number of amateur painters, theater groups, and opera groups is developing. There are, it seems, quite a few weekend Valkyries. Of some 750 opera-producing groups in the United States, only 35 to 40 are fully professional. Statistics on museum attendance also reveal a remarkable growth. From 1952 to 1962, the number of visits to museums increased by well over 100 per cent.

This is a spectacular development and should not be dismissed out of hand. It reflects a remarkable expansion of activity in certain fields, even if the figures have probably been inflated to some extent by improved statistical coverage and enthusiastic reporting. This is probably still the case, even if we take into account that the figures fail to indicate the amount of time actually devoted to amateur painting, and so forth. What is recorded is the number of people saying that they paint on an amateur basis, with no specification of the time during which they indulge in this pursuit. We would, perhaps, expect a rise in these numbers. At a certain income level, a person may take up painting and is then reported as an amateur painter. As income continues to rise, new activities are added and less time — but still some time — may be devoted to painting. He remains on the lists, however, as an amateur painter. In this way, the numbers rise without there necessarily being any rise in total time.

Various statistics aside, it seems reasonable to remain skeptical of the culture boom. Sociologists who have tried to interpret their observations of everyday life appear to have reached conclusions more in line with our a priori argument. In Crestwood Heights there is no lively cultural activity. Neither has the "Organization Man," according to Whyte, found any release from work and mundane consumption.

Most of those questioned were conscious that they didn't read enough good books about something besides business, and some executives went out of their way to berate themselves on that score.

But where, the executive asks, can he find time? Much as he might like to read more history or take in more plays, he looks on this as too marginal, too little relevant to his career to warrant making the time. His judgment is debatable on this point, but that is another story. The fact is that he doesn't see much relationship, and thus, as with the long-deferred project to build a boat with the boys, he will keep on planning that reading he hopes to get around to. One of these days.

And Now a Few Words on Religion

What has happened as regards the time spent in religious pursuits — an important form of spiritual cultivation? In the United States, if not in Europe, one encounters a new wave of religious interest. This would seem to mean that religious activities have succeeded in competing for time, whereas we should have expected the reverse situation, owing to the low goods intensity characteristic of spiritual exercises. The explanation could obviously lie in a marked swing in people's interest, their attention having been attracted to a steadily increasing extent to things religious. It is also possible that the statistics underlying such claims of a religious revival are exaggerated. They could be the results of mere wishful thinking on the part of those compiling the reports. The latter would seem in fact to be the case, if one can believe the investigation made by Charles Y. Glock and Rodney Stark.

It seems in practice as if the increasing pressure of time had not failed to affect religious life. W. W. Schroeder and V. Obenhaus, for instance, found that such features of congregational life as lectures and bazaars had greatly declined. Changes have been noted even in more sacred matters. As Gary Becker points out, "Reform Judaism in the United States has fewer religious holidays and much shorter and less frequent religious services than the more traditional Orthodox have." In the case of Sweden, the average length of sermons seems to have declined. In the Stockholm morning newspaper that announces all coming sermons, exhortations to attend church are customarily carried in advertisement form. On at least one occasion it has been emphasized that sermons are "of reasonable length" and thus "adapted to the modern individual." Such announcements customarily close with the exhortation: "You owe yourself Sunday's hours in church." *

As the pressure of time becomes acute, it has actually happened — if not in Sweden at least in Canada — that the priest has shortened the liturgy. Let us quote from *Crestwood Heights,* where the following very revealing observations were made.

The special tempo that builds up in the non-familiar institutions is noteworthy. The rigid schedule which service-club luncheons follow is well known: so many minutes for lunch — the late-comers must hurry, or sing with their pudding; so many minutes for singing and announcements; and a strict twenty minutes for the speaker. The same emphasis on precision, overshadowed by a general atmosphere of haste, may be noted in the fashionable congregations of the churches which circle Crestwood Heights.

The analysis is underpinned by observations made on different visits to church.

The moment the last prayer was said, everyone stood up and seemed in a great hurry to leave the church, and as the lady sitting beside me seemed particularly anxious to get by me, I had little time to look around. Outside again, I noticed there was little loitering or conversation and

* The pressure of time has probably also affected the length of political speeches. Only in poor countries like Cuba is it conceivable that the head of state should make speeches lasting several hours. Election speeches used necessarily to be long if they were to be successful; now they have been cut to a few pithy demands for improvements.

every one seemed instead to head straight for his car and drive away.

So that the service should not last longer than usual (in spite of the special ceremony and the delay in starting) at two points in the service the minister announced that the singing, first of the *Venite* and then of the *Benedictus,* would be omitted.

And on another occasion:

The hymns, readings, in fact the whole service, were conducted quickly and seemed to be rigidly limited to one hour. No one said 'Good morning' on the way out. Ushers along with everyone else seemed to be in a hurry to get their coats on and be away.

CHAPTER IX

Savings and the Allocation of Time

Money you may waste.
Money regain;
Pile it in your chest,
And thus retain.
Now time, time, alas,
Once it has elapsed,
Never comes again;
No seal whatever,
Lock or bolt could ever
Make it remain.

J. O. Wallin

One Assumption Less

A person's consumption is not always as great as his income from work. If he saves a certain proportion of his income from work, or pays interest on previous loans, then his consumption will be lower than his income. If he enjoys an income from capital, or if he consumes capital assets, then his consumption will be greater than his income from work. If consumption differs from earned income in this way, then the allocation of time will differ from what it is on the assumption so far made that all income is earned income and that all such income is consumed.

Simply to understand the main principles of how time is allocated, it is perhaps unnecessary to take these circumstances into account. Yet, it is worth the effort to bring in these complications. We find, namely, that the allocation of time not only adjusts passively to saving, but — and this is of great interest — that saving is actively used as a means of influencing the allocation of time between different periods. Even if one obviously cannot accumulate time as one piles up money, one can by saving achieve at least a certain intertemporal reallocation in use of time.

Taxes and state benefits cause consumption to deviate from earned income, and this too affects the allocation of time. The most striking consequence is that taxes reduce the degree of specialization, i.e., work time is cut down in favor of personal work of various kinds (as long as the latter type of work remains untaxed). In economic theory, where a rough division is made into work time and free time, this change in the use of time is concealed. The encroachments of the public sector bring about a passive adjustment in the use of time. Taxes, unlike savings, are not used as a means of changing the allocation of time. This makes the effects of taxes less interesting, and we will, therefore, devote our attention to the interplay between savings and allocation of time.

The Mutual Determination of Savings and Time Allocation

The motives for saving are obviously legion. People may wish to save for the benefit of surviving family members. They may want to save in order to provide their children with a good education. They may save from general precautionary motives. Or they may wish to use saving and the running down of assets — dissaving — as a method of reaching a preferred pattern of consumption, differing from the actual flow of their income over the years.

Whatever the motives, saving and dissaving — and the returns of savings — will cause consumption to differ from work income. The allocation of time will thus be affected. However, a much more important possibility is that the propensity for saving is determined in a context of decisions concerning time allocation. If this is the case, it would be possible to understand the motives for saving more fully and to acquire insights into the saving process, by application of the arguments set forth in this essay.

It can be shown that there is, in fact, such a mutual relationship between saving and the allocation of time. We noticed it first when discussing household decision-making and found that the adoption of expenditure routines is a widely used method of saving time. People acquire spending habits, rather than reconsider all the possibilities on every occasion. Furthermore, a given pattern of consumption is accompanied by a certain way of living, reflected in the amounts of time that an individual allocates to his various consumption goods. Both these kinds of habits will dampen the expenditure response to changes in the environment, including changes in income and wealth. Consumers are likely to react to such changes with a certain lag. These lags will result in saving and dissaving, as the case may be. Saving becomes residual. This is one way in which the interplay between the allocation of time and savings can be seen. However, there is also a second mechanism, and one that happens to be much more important. This mechanism has to do with the advantages of a long run stability in the proportions between consumption goods and consumption time.

The Factor Proportions Theory of Why People Save

Considerations of what is required for an efficient combination of enjoyment time and consumption goods in the output of pleasure provide the basis for a new savings theory, which will be suggested here. Assume that an individual wishes to make his material pleasures as great as possible over his life period and that he is indifferent to when during this period he consumes. Then, if he has a constant number of hours per day for enjoyment purposes throughout his life, it will be efficient to maintain a constant level of consumption. Savings and dissavings will be used to even out consumption if income varies. He would not be maximizing total utility if the proportions between the two inputs in pleasure production — goods and time — were not kept constant.* In this respect, his situation is identical with that of

* More exactly, consumption *for enjoyment* should be kept constant. If we assume that consumption *for maintenance* is proportional with consumption for enjoyment, the analysis outlined here holds true. However, there may be swings in maintenance costs. Most typically, medical expenditure — mainte-

any producer. If a manufacturer wants to maximize ouptut over a period, and he has a constant amount of labor at his disposal through that period, it would be inefficient not to spread the available capital resources evenly over the period.

However, it need not be the case that an individual has a constant number of hours for consumption purposes at his disposal over the years. Efficient savings behavior will then be different. If the individual wishes to maintain the same level of utility each year, he must now vary his consumption in the opposite direction to the changes in consumption time. The size of these countervariations will depend upon the possibility of substituting time for goods in consumption.

It might, of course, be asked why time for consumption purposes would vary. In order to keep the factor proportions stable, it would seem to be efficient not to have such variations over the years. This would also be the case if there were no changes in earning capacity. At a period during a person's life span when earning capacity is relatively low, it is advantageous to work shorter hours than when it is high. As age advances, earning capacity usually declines. This fact is recognized in the institution of retirement. If the individual is not to enjoy a higher level of living during retirement than during active working life, he should, during his active life, maintain a higher consumption, in order to offset the shorter time available for this purpose.* But there are shifts in earning capacity also during active life. When the earning capacity is relatively high, it pays to reduce enjoyment time below average in order to make money for the future purposes.† In order, however, not to re-

nance of the body — may shift. Similarly, costs for the maintenance of other durables may be erratic. Furthermore, it is consumption, not consumption expenditure, that should be constant. Part of consumption expenditure — purchases of durables — may shift. In a more ambitious analysis all these complications would have to be considered.

*This adjustment problem is complicated by such factors as a probably declining capacity to enjoy consumption goods and an increasing need of resources not for enjoyment but for the maintenance of particular consumption goods, aging bodies.

†This gives one more reason why high income earners may well work longer hours than average income earners.

duce the level of living below average during that period, an increase in consumption must offset the decline in enjoyment time. It is interesting, in this context, to note the difference in the effect on work effort between a permanent increase in earning capacity and a temporary one. A permanent increase, as we have noted in Chapter III, may well reduce the work effort, whereas a temporary one, owing to the possibility of saving, is bound to increase the work effort. This difference, it seems, is not sufficiently recognized in economists' discussions of the effect of changes in the wage level on work effort. In economic theory, only the effects of permanent income changes on work effort are analyzed. In fact, temporary changes are just as important.

As we see, it can be misleading always to talk of savings as dependent on income. Income itself will be determined as one part of the overall allocation of time. There is a simultaneous determination of hours of work, of consumption time and of savings, as a way of changing time allocation over the years. It is surely a misrepresentation to treat income and hours of work as somewhat preordained and then to study what fraction of that income is saved. At the very least this omits important steps in the analysis.

To elaborate this proposition, let us assume that an individual has made an equilibrium allocation of his time into a certain number of hours for work, maintenance, and consumption. If he now decides to save a certain fraction of his income, the previous allocation of time no longer represents an equilibrium. There will be some time unaccounted for. This time is what would have been absorbed in consuming the goods that the money saved would have bought. Alternatively, we can say that the commodity intensity of available enjoyment time has fallen and is thus reduced below the previous and equilibrium level. Some of the enjoyment time available will be allocated anew in some fashion, thereby raising the commodity intensity of the remaining hours. Part of the time will go into work. Income will thus be higher. Out of this higher income, a certain fraction will be saved. This will again leave a certain amount of time unaccounted for — and so on, until the process converges on a new equilibrium allocation of time. In this equilibrium, savings are not a function of income: income and savings are simultaneously determined in a process of time allocation. Using the same reasoning, we can analyze the effects on time allocation and savings of changes in the wage rate, both temporary and permanent.

Of course, the fact that there is a simultaneous determination of work time, income, and savings does not mean that it could not be of great interest, for a number of reasons, to know how much of actual income is saved. When we try to measure this statistically, we do measure savings as a fraction of income in equilibrium, the time allocation process described an equilibrium brought about by the above. However, it seems important not to lose sight of the fact that income and savings are simultaneously determined.

It could, of course, be argued that income is in fact independently determined, since at first glance it appears that most people have difficulties in varying their hours of work. However, this is hardly correct. Even if we think only of hours of paid work, there is considerable flexibility, at least when the labor market is not disturbed by underemployment. Overtime, moonlighting, and the participation in paid work by married women represent opportunities for income adjustments, according to the equilibrium formula of the individual. But there is also room for variations in income and expenditures through changes in the number of maintenance tasks undertaken individually. By increasing the amount of such home production, an individual can raise both the amount of consumption and savings above what they would be if he had access only to the money he earned through paid work.

It must not be overlooked that what we have stated here as to savings and time allocation are criteria of efficient behavior and not necessarily propositions about actual behavior. It may be advantageous to combine consumption goods and enjoyment time in certain proportions over the years. But from our discussion of decision-making by households, it should be clear that such an efficiency criterion is built on an assumption of perfect knowledge and zero information costs. In reality the situation is different. We must expect that people will not systematically try to estimate their future earnings. There is quite a widespread use of current earnings as an index of the future situation. In such a case, actual behavior will differ from what would be efficient behavior under perfect knowledge. In certain situations, however, income changes will evidently be looked upon as temporary. Savings and consumption will then change only to offset the utility decline, which would otherwise be the result of shorter time for consumption purposes, when work hours expand as a result of improved temporary earning capacity. It is also likely that individuals will at least make an effort to evaluate their future situation and gear their consumption to this estimate, using saving and dissaving as a tool.

Existing Savings Theories

As noted by way of introduction, a variety of motives for saving can be discerned. In the economic literature there has been an extensive discussion of what determines savings behavior. It would be well beyond the intentions of this essay to review this literature. Yet, since no consensus has been reached, it may be interesting to explore the main hypotheses that have been advanced, with the intention of seeing whether the time allocation approach has any bearing on the relative position of these rival theories.

In order to denote the propensity to save, saving is expressed as a fraction of income. The size of this fraction is likely to depend upon many factors of a sociological or psychological nature, in which income itself is usually considered as the decisive element. Individual and group differences are not taken into account, insofar as they are not reflected in income itself. Thus the fraction of current income that is saved will, it is argued, depend upon income. Unfortunately, people mean different things by this income, which will determine the propensity to save. We can distinguish among three different approaches.

a. The absolute income hypothesis. This hypothesis asserts that the fraction of current income that is saved will depend upon current income. As current income rises, the power to gratify various savings motives will rise and rise more than proportionally with the rise in income.

b. The relative income hypothesis. In its original version this hypothesis suggests that the proportion of income saved depends on the current income of the individual, in relation to average income in the society. The higher this relation, the higher will be the proportion saved. The relative position of the individual on the income ladder is what matters. The rationale of this idea is that people wish to conform. They want to keep up with the Joneses, but not to outdo them.

On the basis of this argument, it is possible to give the hypothesis a slightly different form. If individuals wish to emulate their neighbors and also strive to increase their level of living, it is likely that they will raise consumption as income goes up and be unwilling to reduce it if the income goes down. What will then determine consumption is current income in relation to the highest level of income — or, as has also been suggested, the highest level of consumption — previously reached by the individual.

c. The permanent income and life-cycle income hypotheses. These hypotheses, almost identical in approach, are built on a distinction between "permanent" and "transitory" income. Permanent income is the average income expected over the life cycle, or whatever shorter planning period may be considered. Similarly, consumption is divided into a permanent and a transitory component. The latter consists of unforeseen expenditures (unusually high medical bills) or fewer expenditures than anticipated (warm weather reducing heating costs). The argument is that permanent consumption is geared to permanent income, the transitory elements being uncorrelated and averaging out overtime. If transitory income is positive and not fully offset by transistory consumption, there will be savings and vice-versa. People try to reach a preferred pattern of consumption which differs from the actual income pattern.

The foremost empirical fact that the rival savings theories are asked to explain is that, on the one hand, cross-section household studies reveal that the higher the measured income, the larger the savings fraction seems to be, while time series, on the other hand, suggest that the fraction of income saved does not rise as average income grows. A simple absolute income hypothesis cannot be used to explain this apparent contradiction. Attempts have been made, however, to prop up the theory by bringing in other factors, which could explain why the savings ratio has not increased with incomes. The relative income theory does manage to show that there might be no contradiction in the results from cross-section and time series data. In the long run, the normal income, to which high and low income earners conform in each period, moves upwards. The life-cycle and permanent income hypotheses can also be used to show that there is no conflict. In cross-section studies, low income cases will be heavily loaded with negative transitory incomes. Savings rates will thus be low. Similarly, high income cases will be loaded with positive transitory incomes. Savings rates will thus be high. In the time series, the permanent incomes have increased. Consumption too has thus increased, leaving the savings fraction constant.

The variety of competing hypotheses means that whatever empirical tests have been undertaken have not been conclusive. It would be interesting if the a priori arguments suggested here as to the role of savings in relationship to time could somewhat reduce the uncertainty. The following comments, which can serve also as a summary, seem to make that possible.

1. The implications of the time allocation theory for consumer behavior yield a priori support to the life-cycle income hypothesis. When income shifts, it will be appropriate for a consumer to use the opportunity of saving, in order to even out consumption.

2. However, income is determined within an overall allocation of time into work time and consumption time. Thus both income and consumption time are likely to shift over the years. Changes in the availability of consumption time should be allowed to influence what proportion of the total life-cycle income is consumed in a particular period. Since, over the life-cycle, the availability of consumption time is inversely related to work time, and thus probably to current income, the proportion of the life-cycle income which is consumed in a given period will tend to vary with current income. The permanent income hypothesis neglects the fact that many transitory income

changes — but not all (for instance, lottery gains) — are due to non-permanent changes in earning capacity which will affect the allocation of time and thus influence savings. These relationships give some support to the predictions of the absolute income hypothesis, if not to the arguments behind that theory.

3. These propositions as to the combination of goods and time over the years must be regarded as prescriptive. Saving and dissaving are required for consumer efficiency. In reality, there will be certain information costs. As we know from our discussion of household decision-making, however, rules of thumb will be used in such situations, since the high cost of acquiring information makes it efficient to do so. This must be expected to influence savings behavior.

4. One principle of decision-making is the formation of expenditure routines and consumption habits. Consumption must for this reason be expected to react with a lag to changes in income and wealth. This can produce the consumer behavior suggested in the relative income hypothesis.

5. A different rule of thumb is to use recent experience as a basis for evaluating permanent income. In this case the permanent income hypothesis might be modified by taking a shorter period than the life cycle as a planning period. But if the planning period becomes very short, with people using current income as an index for permanent income, this approach will collapse into the absolute income hypothesis.

As these points may indicate, it is perhaps possible to give the rival savings theories a unified interpretation within a factor proportions theory of saving — a theory derived from the time allocation approach.

CHAPTER X

Will We Reach a Consumption Maximum?

> I look forward, therefore, in days not
> so very remote, to the greatest change
> which has ever occurred in the material
> environment of life for human beings in
> the aggregate.
>
> J. M. Keynes

Will the Level of Income Rise?

In the first nine chapters we have assumed that the level of productivity will continue steadily to rise. We then tried to investigate what changes in the use of time the resulting scarcity of time would create. We cannot, however, take it for granted that the level of productivity will in fact go on rising. What we must ask ourselves in particular is whether the conclusions so far arrived at suggest in themselves that per capita incomes will no longer continue to increase.

The question as to whether incomes and consumption will reach a certain level, beyond which no further increase is possible, is an ancient one. It has also proved a controversial one, and has led to heated exchanges of opinion. The dispute has dealt with two different reasons why there may be a ceiling to rises in consumption. We can distinguish between an enforced and a voluntary consumption maximum, depending on the type of economic free play that is exhausted.

An Enforced Consumption Maximum

An enforced consumption maximum would occur, if technical progress stopped. Continued investment would then exhaust the fund of available investment opportunities. The productivity of additional capital accumulation would eventually become zero, and only reinvestment would take place. Under these circumstances, income and consumption could no longer rise.

If there is some population growth, there might of course be room for some investment, even in the absence of technical progress. However, this investment could not raise income and consumption per capita. It would only permit the additional labor to be equipped with capital goods so that the same level of living could be extended to the newcomers. If, on balance, natural resources are being depleted, there must actually be a certain amount of technical progress and profitable investment to prevent income and consumption from falling. If, instead, new discoveries more than offset the depletion of known resources, the reverse is of course true.

What the future rate of technical progress will be is largely a matter of conjecture. The classical economists took the attitude that technology would eventually reach a limit and thus tended to think that there would be an enforced consumption maximum. However, the longer technical progress continued, the more reasonable it appeared that it would continue to go on. Nonetheless, the notion of a secular stagnation was not abandoned. Some economists began to argue that, in "mature economies," technical progress would not be fast enough to keep up with the flow of intended savings. *Potential* full employment income might rise, but *actual* income might not. If the wish to save is not matched by the propensity for investing, there will be depressive forces which may cause a tendency to secular stagnation. The savings-investment relationships have, of course, been used to explain cyclical swings. However, they have also been introduced to propose that some long-run difficulties may be encountered in increasing income and consumption. This approach is perhaps most associated with the name of Alvin Hansen, but even J. M. Keynes himself suggested that his own theories imply certain long-run problems. Owing to rapid, perhaps accelerating, technological progress during recent decades, little interest has been given to the possibility that there may eventually be an enforced consumption maximum even of this type.

A Voluntary Consumption Maximum

If goals are fixed, a voluntary consumption maximum will eventually be reached. As income expands, more and more wants will be gratified. Ultimately, the utility of additions to income and consumption would be zero. On the assumption that goals are given, this must be the case. However, what are we to think of the assumption itself?

Some have expressed strong hopes that eventually man will reach a point where he is blessed by satisfaction with his material well-being. In the great Utopian writings, from Sir Thomas More to E. Bellamy, man is not constantly craving for economic betterment, but has reached a material level at which his interests and energies have been diverted to other activities which he deems superior. This was the Good Place to the Utopians. Some of the early economists sympathized with such hopes. In the words of John Stuart Mill, "the best state for the human nature is that in which, while no one is poor, no one desires to be richer, nor has any reasons for fear of being thrust back, by the efforts of others to push themselves forward."

Utopians as well as anti-utopians write to affect rather than predict the future. They need not have been of the opinion that there is actually a limit to human material wants. A number of commentators, however, have been convinced that there would eventually be a consumption maximum. Karl Marx, for instance, thought that sooner or later the rich would become so rich that they would not be able to find any additional frills on which to spend their money. Marx's reasoning depended upon peculiar ideas as to how the income distribution would evolve. But even with the more equal income distribution, which in fact characterizes the opulent countries, the average person, just as the wealthy classes, would eventually become rich enough to hit his head against the ceiling of wants. Keynes, in exploring the "Economic Possibilities for Our Grandchildren," embraced the idea that human beings have material appetites that are satiable. He thus saw a fading away of the basic economic problem, a process however which, as we have already noted, might be troubled by difficulties in maintaining full employment. For the present generation, the best-known adherent to the idea that wants can be exhausted is J. K. Galbraith. The reason why we are not already experiencing this saturation point is, according to him, the "dependence effect." Wants through advertising and emulation come to depend upon output rather than on any need to eliminate scarcity.

In a little-noticed paper, Roy F. Harrod has joined the group of economists who are prepared to recognize the possibility of saturation. The conventional argument against the notion of a saturation of wants is that, after all, even those with extremely high incomes seem to enjoy their high consumption. Envious empiricism confirms this, and introspection yields the conclusion that it would be easy to spend astronomical sums on consumption. Any saturation of wants must, therefore, be so distant that it is idle to speculate about it now.

However, as Harrod points out, this inference is fallacious. The satiation point of a minority is necessarily far above the satiation point of a majority. In other words, saturation will occur when many have reached a certain income, although that same income, earned by only a few, would by no means imply saturation. The main reason for this is that a substantial part of the consumption of income oligarchs is a consumption of personal services, which cannot be duplicated when all earn the same high income. When your income has risen, so has that of your potential servants. The average person can afford no more personal services than he could in the Stone Age. For the income oligarchs, it is easy to spend phenomenal sums on consumption, as maintenance work can be eliminated, and only the pleasant aspects of consumption remain. Mansions and ski huts and the things associated with living in them, and away from them, are more attractive if the owners need not do the washing, sweeping, scraping, polishing, and guarding all by themselves. The ultimate luxury is to be liberated even from the hardships of having to do one's own buying. The consumer's path is then as smooth as it can ever be. Against this background, it is quite consistent to be pleased to accept a considerable increase in one's own income and at the same time to argue that there may be some saturation point if everybody has a high income. An income oligarch possesses an entrance ticket to the Veblen leisure class, but by definition, only a few can have so much more than the average that it enables them to pass the gilded gate.

However, while those approaching economic problems from a philosophical angle have worshipped the prospect of a saturation of wants, others have ridiculed it. Indeed, most people seem to think that wants are inexhaustible. They do not expect the utility of income additions to become zero or even to decline. The idea that there may be some point at which not only the stomach, but the whole body, including head and heart, is fed, if not fed up, is usually denied. John Stuart Mill's views on the bliss of the stagnant state have a queer ring in modern ears. Talk of a consumption maximum is contemptuously referred to as "idealism" or "utopianism" — concepts which have nowadays acquired pejorative overtones as being impractical. These commentators are, of course, honest in their disbelief in a saturation of wants. They are also hostile to the very idea. This is perhaps surprising. We have come to dislike ultimate success. The means have become the end. Dissatisfaction with one's material conditions is regarded as the stimulus of life. Our hopes and ambitions are tied to material "progress." Our enterprising spirit requires it as an outlet. Efforts to achieve economic growth have created their own values and vested interests. Saturation appears as a threat of greater dimensions than a mere problem of economic policy.

This threat — which formerly was not a threat but a promise — is not however taken too seriously. Economists and noneconomists alike take comfort in the fact that people are conspicuously interested in material advancement, even after centuries of what, in fact, has been an accelerating growth of consumption. As new consumption heights are reached, people dare — thank God — to raise their aspiration levels. Whether through advertising or not, the appetite of the mass consumer can always be relied upon to be whetted. Decreasing marginal utility might affect individual commodities but not aggregate consumption. What George Katona has reverently referred to as "the miracle of consumption" will, it is believed, be an even greater miracle a hundred years hence.

A Different Interpretation of Current Trends

Neither the quality of the idea that there will be an enforced consumption maximum on the supply side, nor that of the idea that there will be a voluntary consumption maximum on the demand side, can or will be decided on here. True enough, the supply argument can probably be disregarded at least in a projection for a couple of decades hence. Technical progress shows no signs of tapering off. Similarly, the demand argument is probably unrealistic, as new wants, whether emerging by themselves or engineered, do seem to assert themselves. J. K. Galbraith himself, in enunciating his "dependence principle," accepts that wants are not exhausted. That they are increased through manipulation may be true but, as soon as they are not exhausted, there cannot be a declining utility of income due to a declining urgency of unfulfilled wants.

But even if our needs are infinite and production techniques continue to improve, there is a further possibility of the scope for continued consumption increases becoming exhausted. A time allocation analysis shows this indeed to be the case. The limit need not be set by our resources on the production side or by needs on the consumption side. The decisive factor can instead be a resource on the consumption side, namely time. By the conventional way of looking at things, consumption is instantaneous. The only possible restrictions are the ability to produce and the will to consume. Production is dependent upon technology, and the utility of production on wants. But if the supply of time is limited, and if time is a necessary resource, not only in production but also in consumption, then time will function as a restriction. The degree of utilization of consumption goods declines. Since the price of consumption time increases, the increase in national product is not at fixed prices, even if all prices of goods remain unchanged. The increase in volume of consumption is, therefore, an imperfect measure of the rise in material standards. The increasing scarcity of time will mean that growth in consumption goods, however intensely we may desire to improve our material standard, will provide a dwindling increment to that standard. Since we need not relate the volume of consumption to anything so diffuse as "wants," but to something as measurable as time, it is also possible to reach a definite conclusion on the contribution of consumption increases.

Increases in the volume of consumption might thus give only dwindling increments to well-being, for two different reasons: wants can gradually become less pressing or the possibilities of utilizing consumption increases can become smaller, owing to an increased scarcity of time. The latter case, unlike the former, does not presuppose any decline in the intensity of our desire to acquire further material improvements.

Certain economists have discussed more or less explicitly the eventuality that limited time can entail a decline in the pleasure derived from income increases. The writer who has done this most clearly is Roy F. Harrod. The upshot of Harrod's argument is that an increasing scarcity of time makes it increasingly less attractive to acquire further goods which have to be maintained in various ways. To Harrod's remarks we need add only the observation that even actual consumption takes time, a fact which reinforces the tendency for consumption increases to provide a dwindling utility on the margin. Apart from the need for this addendum, the only weakness in Harrod's argument is that he fails to notice that a declining utility of income increases caused by time scarcity does *not* imply the gradual satisfaction of all desires.

In the literature on fiscal policy, at least one other writer has taken into account the consequences of an increasing scarcity of time. In trying to construct a just system of taxation on a scientific basis, it seemed reasonable for us to investigate how far income increases provide a declining increment of people's enjoyment.

In a well-known paper of 1913, J. S. Chapman tried to prove that the marginal utility of income does *not* decline. In the process, he made the observation that rich people are less careful about their cents than poor people. This habit of the rich had sometimes been taken as a sign of a lower marginal utility of income than that of the poor. Chapman rejected this inference. He said that, although the rich may appear less careful about their money, this is due simply to the fact that their time is so valuable that it would be uneconomic for them to reflect much about cents.

Chapman's point is interesting as a rare example of an economist applying the rationale of increasing irrationality. However, it is questionable to use this idea to reject the possibility of there being a declining utility of income additions. Chapman is right in that casualness with money among the rich need not indicate any exhaustion of wants. However, it is erroneous to think that this casualness does not indicate a lower marginal utility of money due to time reasons. The rationality of increasing irrationality and the declining utility of income for time reasons are both implications of the same basic idea, namely the increasing scarcity of time. One cannot use one implication of an idea to reject another implication of the same basic idea. Indeed, the declining quality of decision-making is one of the reasons that income additions will result in declining additions to utility. The confusion in Chapman's argument is due to his failure to distinguish between the two different possible causes of a declining utility of income additions. He should have concluded that, although there may be a declining utility of income additions, this does not mean that the wants of the high income earners are satisfied to a higher degree.

The Time Constraint and the Likelihood of a Consumption Maximum

If income increments lead to smaller and smaller additions to material welfare, owing to the increasing scarcity of time, does this mean that we shall in time be confronted with a consumption maximum? If wants are gradually satisfied and increases in income reduce marginal utility of consumption to zero, we shall be faced with a consumption maximum. If income increases cannot continue, owing to a stagnant technology, then we shall also be faced with a consumption ceiling. But what happens if the restriction is a growing scarcity of time?

Harrod believed, as we have seen, that the increasing scarcity of time would lead to our gradually losing interest in further income increases. Harrod reasoned, however, as if the declining limit utility of income increases were equivalent to our wants being successively exhausted. This lack of clarity, or error, in his reasoning can easily have led to an incorrect conclusion.

In Table 1, we saw that a consumption maximum will be reached abruptly if goods claim a certain given time per unit for maintenance and enjoyment. We have since shown that great opportunities probably exist to substitute time with goods in both maintenance and consumption, and that this is in fact done when goods become cheaper in relation to time. This substitution is reflected in a gradually dwindling increment of utility from increases in the volume of goods. This possibility of substituting goods for time means that we need not be faced with the situation that the utility of further income increases reaches zero. There is, therefore, nothing to prevent a consumer from trying to make the best of the situation and continuing to raise his consumption and thus his well-being. We have assumed, after all, that technological progress is still being made, so that we can, if we want, increase production. We have also said that the intensity of our aspirations to achieve material improvements is probably as strong as ever. Individuals will, therefore, desire to increase their consumption with a view to raising their material standard. There will be no conflict either between the desire to increase well-being and the possibility of doing so by raising consumption or between the desire to raise consumption and the technological possibility of raising production. We see here how important it is to distinguish between cases in which we have a declining utility of income increases owing to an exhaustion of wants and when it is owing to an increasing scarcity of time. In these two cases, we reach entirely different conclusions about what sort of efforts will be made to raise the level of consumption.

In actual fact we see that, under the conditions outlined, there will be an acceleration of efforts to raise the level of consumption. If a person desires to increase his material well-being by a certain percentage every year, then the volume of his consumption must be pushed up by a higher and higher percentage every year. This is because a given percentage increase in consumption offers a dwindling percentage addition to material standards. If the consumption increase were to be effected by a given percentage each year, then his material standard would improve only at a declining rate. In this situation, we can expect great importance to be attached to economic growth in economic policy and to economic efforts in the individual's structuring of his existence. The fact that we are so desperately interested in economic growth, therefore, cannot be taken as indicating in any way that it is unreasonable to speak of a declining utility of consumption increases. The difficulties of increasing our material standard by pushing up our consumption volume will be experienced by most of us as an economic problem. The only known medicine for economic problems is to raise incomes. We can, therefore, expect the interest in economic growth to be great even when the utility of consumption increases reaches a very low level. It is possible that we shall desire economic growth, even if the utility of consumption increases were zero.

The increase in the scarcity of time occurs as a continuous process. It is, therefore, not easily made the basis for a division of the economic growth process into clearly separated periods. Even so, it can be instructive to divide the economic process into three periods that have different characteristics, as described with the help of our time allocation analysis. The first period is the constructive phase of growth. The necessary material conditions for a satisfactory use of time are created. Time becomes more scarce, but at first only by economic free time being absorbed in a meaningful way. The scarcity of time increases even beyond that, but without the time devoted to culture decreasing, for example. Nor is the scarcity so great that disruptions occur in the form of an inefficient flurry in the use of time or in a strong orientation to goods in consumption at the cost of human coexistence. The poor countries are only at the beginning of this period.

The second period is that of decadence. The phase of vulgarization is characterized by a marked scarcity of time. The utility of further increases in the average income has, in other words, fallen considerably. The demand for further improvements in material conditions, however, is still strong. As a result, economic questions occupy a dominant position both in political life and in the private lives of individuals. Economic improvement comes in this way to be regarded no longer as a means to a goal, but as a goal in itself. The form taken by efforts made during this phase of decadence will be studied in Chapter XI. It is a question of judgment whether the rich countries have yet entered this period, or if so, how deeply they have penetrated it.

Then there is a third period — the phase of reformation — which may or may not come about. During this period, the idea of progress will acquire a new content. Owing to the scarcity of time, it will be extremely difficult to raise the level of human well-being by raising the level of consumption. People will acquire new purposes. In Chapter XII we shall briefly discuss these ultimate economic developments.

CHAPTER XI

The Period of Decadence

While the economic condition of countries
is bad, men care for Political Economy,
which may tell us how it is to be improved;
when that condition is improved, Political
Economy ceases to have the same popular interest.

Walter Bagehot

An Unexpected Urge

Enormous attention is devoted today to economic growth. Professors and politicians are immersed in economic theory and economic policy. Moreover, our very interest in these matters is growing. It is only since the war, in fact, that people have begun consciously and systematically to concern themselves with methods of achieving a high growth rate.

It may seem surprising that the interest in economic growth should thus increase in step with the level of incomes. As suggested by the above quotation from Bagehot, it was previously imagined that economic considerations would gradually decline in importance, finally perhaps to disappear altogether. John Stuart Mill, as we have seen, also believed that people would in time be able to rest from their economics. Even J. M. Keynes, in the years between the wars, could proclaim that the economic problem would disappear in the foreseeable future. Statements of this sort are no longer made. They would seem frivolous. Writers emphasize instead how vital it is that we push up the rate of growth. To quote Moses Abramovitz: "Few things have been more common in recent economics literature and in political pronouncements than expressions of dissatisfaction with the pace of U.S. economic growth, accompanied with ringing demands that we 'can and must' speed up the pace of our development."

One or another writer has admittedly pointed to this growing concern for economic growth with some astonishment, but without apparently finding any difficulties in explaining the phenomenon. A long list of explanations has been offered, beyond the possibility that people quite simply want to increase the rate of their consumption growth. Greater resources are needed, it has been said, so that more help can be extended to the poorer countries. More resources are needed to increase aid to the needy minorities in the rich countries themselves. *The Other America* exists, and not only in the United States. Both of these pious aims would be convincing enough, if only it could be shown that increases in welfare were actually devoted to such ends. This, however, is doubtful. There is a certain apathy in the rich countries toward increasing their aid to the emerging countries. As regards the poor minorities, the new poverty is pathological rather than the result of a low productivity. It has emerged for the very reason that not everybody could make direct use of productivity increases by his own input. Nor have these poor benefited indirectly to any great extent from increased welfare via state aid. It is typical of social policy, even in a country like Sweden, that it is the interests of the majorities, not the small, needy minorities, which are catered to. The chronically sick, the disabled, and the mentally disturbed are some of the minorities which are given handouts instead of being the prime beneficiaries of the welfare state.

It has been claimed that greater resources are required for defense, education, and medical care. This may be true, but it hardly explains why the interest in growth is increasing. In the Soviet Union and the United States, the defense argument probably plays a major role. But it can hardly be the driving force behind this interest in growth, since the latter is equally strong in countries like Sweden and Germany.

It is asserted that more resources are needed for cultural development. The cultural optimists have declined in number, but there still surely exist those who dare to see economic growth as a means of promoting cultural development. In the same way, many surely believe that economic growth is needed to increase the amount of free time and reduce the hectic pace of our existence. Even if growth in reality had the reverse effect — culture time is pressed down, and the pace of life increases — the view currently held could naturally have its effect. But it is still difficult to see why these aims should lead to an increasing interest in growth.

A country must maintain a high rate of economic development to hold its own in the "growth Olympics." This is a view put forward by many, and it is naturally true enough in itself. But it fails to explain why any such competition between countries has ever emerged. Similarly, it is sometimes argued that economic growth is needed to give expression to people's drive to self-aggrandizement. In Keynes's words:

> . . . dangerous human proclivities can be canalised into comparatively harmless channels by the existence of opportunities for money-making and private wealth, which, if they cannot be satisfied in this way, may find their outlet in cruelty, the reckless pursuit of personal power and authority, and other forms of self-aggrandisement. It is better that a man should tyrannise over his bank balance than over his fellow-citizens.

However valid this observation may be, it too fails to explain why these forces should find an outlet just in economic progress. Nor can it explain why the interest in growth is increasing.

It has been claimed that economists have interested themselves in growth only more recently, because they had not previously solved the difficult problems involved in business cycles. That economists should have tried first to cure the primary diseases before attacking the more sophisticated problems seems only reasonable. But it hardly seems reasonable cause for all the laymen to have been fired with this increased concern for growth.

Yet another explanation for the increasing interest in economic progress is the recognition that a general insight into the fact that welfare cannot in the long run be increased by the *redistribution* of resources has only just been achieved. Increased material resources can instead be achieved only by increased productivity. Such a revised way of thinking may have played its part, but it seems in itself a somewhat thin explanation.

The decisive driving force behind the increasing interest in economic growth is probably, quite simply, a striving to raise material standards. People want higher and higher consumption, faster and faster increases in standards. This is hardly any revelation. What is surprising is simply people's unwillingness to admit the truth. The other motives customarily adduced are probably rationalizations, with no independent life of their own. Insofar as they are not contradicted by the use to which our growing resources are actually put, they are simply reflections on various planes of the consumers' desire to increase their material well-being in all conceivable ways.

We can claim that there is an interest in increasing consumption more and more quickly, without this contradicting the thesis that the increments provided to well-being by income increases are declining. As long as additions to income have a declining utility on the margin, owing not to the exhaustion of desires but to the increasing scarcity of time, the result will be precisely a growing interest in economic growth. In order to achieve material improvements — which we have a strong desire to do — we must steadily increase the additions to our incomes.

The sharper the conflict between the declining utility of additional income and the rising desires to increase well-being, the greater propensity there will be for increasing economic growth by all possible means. Cultural development, other than as a luxury for the few, has perhaps never been more than a dream, but this is now being openly confessed. Economic growth has become an overriding end — not a means. As many have observed, there is a certain cost of progress in the form of various institutional changes that have to be accepted in order to permit the growth process. The higher the level of incomes, the readier people become to pay these costs in order to ensure still more rapid consumption increases. It is possible to employ methods that are actually destructive in order to bring about economic growth, i.e., means that sooner or later prove to entail a lower material standard. We shall be giving below various examples of how this strong, sometimes destructive, concern with growth is reflected.

Growth Mania at the Individual Level

A rising general level of productivity can lead to work time being either reduced or prolonged, depending on how difficult it is to substitute goods for time in consumption. We are thus unable to decide a priori whether or not actual work time is above the optimal level, i.e., the level that would lead to achievement of the greatest possible material satisfaction. If one could show that actual work time lay above the optimum, this would provide an interesting case of growth mania.

Even if no definite conclusions can be drawn from the way in which working hours have actually developed, it may be of interest to note that no further reductions in working hours seem to be taking place in the United States. This *could* mean that people were dissatisfied with the additional well-being produced by their income increases; they thus wish to increase the size of these additions to income, and they do this through more intensive work. Typically enough, we encourage even so a myth that working hours are being steadily reduced. In this way, we get both our consumption goods and a feeling that we have more time in which to use them. The statistics, however, give a different picture.

Let us look at developments in the United States. Average weekly hours in the latter part of the nineteenth century can be estimated at well over 60. In 1909, the average weekly hours of production workers in manufacturing — as calculated by the U.S. Bureau of Labor Statistics — stood at 51. By 1929 they had fallen to 44. During the Great Depression and World War II, there were swings which have special explanations. However, *since the first postwar period there has been no further reduction in the work week*. There have been minor ups and downs, due probably to cyclical changes, but the movements have been around a flat trend line at just over 40 hours per week.

This picture is confirmed if we look at a different set of figures. While the average workweek is calculated by the U.S. Bureau of Labor Statistics from payroll data on numbers of hours worked and number of employees, the Census Bureau at regular intervals conducts sample studies of individuals and their work hours. The advantage of these data for our purposes is that they make it possible to see more clearly the role of part time and overtime. The spreading practice of part-time work among women and teenagers is causing a reduction in the average work week as statistically measured, without this really signifying any decline in work input; especially as many of those now working part time were previously not gainfully employed. As to overtime, this would be included in the average work week. However, if overtime takes the form of multiple job-holding, this will, peculiarly enough, reduce the average work week, if — as is usual — the second job is part time.

Again the conclusion we can derive is that, on an average, the weekly hours of the full-time, nonfarm work force have remained constant during the postwar period at a level of about 45 hours. If we look at components of the over-all data, we find that in this period, the number of people working more than 48 hours a week has doubled or risen from 13 per cent of the work force in 1948 to 20 per cent in 1965. Some 5 per cent of the work force holds more than one job. For white married men the figure is substantially higher. At least over the last decade there has been no decline in multiple job-holding. As this practice cannot have been widespread until a decline in the work week began, it is reasonable to conclude that this phenomenon has instead been gradually increasing. Some estimates indicate also that multiple job-holding has doubled since 1950.

To render an exhaustive account of changes in the work week, we would have to allow for a number of additional problems. Changes in absences due to sickness, in number of hours paid for but not worked (vacations), in travel time to the work place, in definitions of work time and pauses, and in the total family work week (as opposed to individual work week) are examples of further complications that would have to be considered. However, for our purpose, we need not dig more deeply into the labor statistics. The main conclusion seems to be sufficiently clear from crude data: the reduction in work time has ceased.

This conclusion differs strongly with the conventional wisdom by which there is a marked fall in work time and by which continued productivity increases will soon bring about, say, a thirty-hour work week. It is possible to see a number of reasons why the view that a dramatic decline is occurring in work hours should be widespread. Most important probably is that people simply think in terms of what has happened since the Industrial Revolution and forget to explore the direction of changes over recent years. There is also a human tendency to see only what we expect to see. In order to make it even more difficult to note the differences between facts and expectations, we tend also to make reductions in the legal work week — reductions which are then misinterpreted to mean reductions in the actual work week. The decline in the proportion of people engaged in agriculture — where hours are substantially above average — may also create an impression of a decline in the work week by what is only a change in the composition of the work force.

Some people work long hours, in order to become income oligarchs and to obtain access to those pleasures which, as Harrod noted, are necessarily reserved for a minority, no matter how much average productivity rises. Perhaps, to an even greater extent, long hours are the result of a fondness for work, rather than for the income in which work results. Compulsive work may be substituted for compulsory work. A still greater number of people, perhaps, are work maniacs, who try to keep haunting, disturbing thoughts at a distance. However, most people will not curtail the work week, in spite of increases in productivity, for the simple reason that they are not satisfied with the increases in consumption that would then be possible. This would mean that, owing to a declining utility of additional income combined with an urge to improve the level of well-being, people are lured into a misallocation of time, thus becoming the victims of growth obsession. The fact that we so ardently encourage the myth of the declining work week indicates that there is a vague feeling of uncertainty about the propriety of the present allocation of time. Some, like Bertrand Russell, actually feel called upon to speak up In Praise of Idleness.

Growth Mania at the National Level

However, for the harried leisure class it must appear particularly attractive to obtain higher incomes, without having to work long hours. We must thus expect there to be a strong emphasis on economic growth through increases in overall productivity. The stimulation of economic growth becomes a primary goal in the efforts of a nation.

One way of promoting economic growth may be to encourage the study of economics on both the academic and less exalted levels. At least in Sweden, there has been, during the postwar period, a great expansion in the number of students exposed to economics courses. In this way, people come to understand what the requirements for growth are. Economic policies need not be hampered by misguided obstructionist behavior. People can see the economic costs of their various idiosyncrasies. The observation has often been made that, although there is much talk of economic development in the underdeveloped countries, they are often not prepared to pay the price of progress. They seem unwilling to accept deep-going changes in the structure of their societies — changes which are necessarily part of economic development. In the advanced countries, the situation is different. We have no unslaughtered holy cows. The population of human beings and animals alike is sized according to the requirements of growth. We are steadily more inclined to see things in purely economic terms. Waste and inefficiency will be increasingly abhorred. Yet — as an exercise in paradox — we can at the same time recall that the rationale of increasing irrationality will make our actual use of resources increasingly ill-considered and seemingly irrational. An interesting and somewhat forbidding manifestation of growth obsession is the extent to which we are willing to make even ideological sacrifices in the name of growth. We would allow democracy to be diluted to ensure economic efficiency, as it might be through executive supremacy and national planning. Even if we did think that this would bring us onto the road to serfdom, this price of progress would be accepted. An age whose intellectuals speak of "human investment," where those of earlier periods spoke of "the dignifying experience of education," has changed its ideals.

It should be noted that, as the Communist countries advance, they too seem to be prepared to sacrifice more and more of their ideology, in order to secure continued economic growth. Business incentives of a capitalist type are gradually being introduced, although, according to their dogma, this is a sure way of debasing the individual. If the Chinese are still dogmatic, it is because they can afford to be, owing to the high utility of even small income additions at their present low levels of consumption.

From an engineering of ideals, it is but a small step to a doctoring of data. The great interest in economic growth has resulted in index folly. As is well known, statistical difficulties make it impossible to construct an index of the gross national product which faithfully records changes in our material well-being. Yet, some kind of index is required for people to be able to register what they might otherwise be unable to notice. But once an index, with all its imperfections, has been constructed, it assumes an importance in its own right. In order to wage political campaigns under the battle cry "you never had it so good," governments will take actions designed to push up the index figures rather than the well-being of the population. Similarly, the opposition party or parties will closely watch the movement of the index to find openings to criticize the ineffectiveness of economic policy. Such behavior is not the result of ill will among politicians. It faithfully reflects the fact that people want rapid economic progress and that the index, supposedly, records the rate of progress. It is the statistical scorecard that counts and not the nonquantified or nonquantifiable ingredients in life.

It is particularly interesting to note that the index we all study takes no account of the time devoted to enjoying the consumption goods acquired. To achieve rapid increases in the index, governments have, therefore, helped to maintain working hours at a high level.

There are many more pleasant things that do not enter into the statistics. Pure air and clean water we appreciate, but such utilities are not on the tally. The same is true of the pleasures derived from enjoying the beauty of nature. As an aspect of growth obsession manifested in index folly, we should thus expect little interest in these attractions, compared with solid investments in plant and equipment. This is indeed the case. We choose not to listen to the mute message of *The Silent Spring*. In this way we manage, at least temporarily, to keep up the registered rate of growth. But we also manage to keep down the well-being of the nation.

It should not be denied that the destruction of natural resources, such as air and water, has met with increasing opposition during the last decade. However, this is due to a surprisingly high extent to the fact that a further destruction of these resources would in the end prove detrimental to the statistically recorded consumption itself. Our civilization runs an obvious risk of being smothered in smog. According to Professor Neiburger, former President of the American Meteorological Society: "All civilization will pass away not from sudden cataclysm like a nuclear war, but from gradual suffocation in its own wastes." Statements like this are not rare, but they are rarely listened to. The day this paragraph was first drafted, *The New York Times* carried an article on the extreme seriousness of the air pollution in New York. A couple of days later — Thanksgiving, 1966 — the situation became critical.

However, in spite of all our efforts to speed up the rate of growth and to persuade people that the rate of growth is high, the additions to income need not be regarded as satisfactory. More than is provided will be desired, in order to obtain the required addition to pleasure. If there is dissatisfaction with the presents provided by growth, there will be one more kind of manifestation of growth obsession, in this case in the form of "operation bootstraps." This we experience at the national level in the form of government spending in excess of government income, even when such fiscal policies would not be prompted by Keynesian efforts to cure underemployment.

Our interest in growth takes all forms — possible and impossible.

CHAPTER XII

Economic Ultimates

Surely, my friends, plenty of bacon is
good and indispensable, but, I doubt,
that you will never get even bacon by
aiming only at that.

Thomas Carlyle

The Naive Visions

Where is economic growth taking us? Will the demand for economic progress ever be entirely satisfied? If not, why not? If such demands cannot be met, how will our economy and our society develop?

These are challenging and important questions. It is hardly remarkable that they have not been answered. It is strange, however, that they are rarely posed. Among laymen and economists alike, there is an absence of debate as to the purpose of our economic efforts and the content of our economic future. Seductive economists extrapolate the general level of income and create visions of a general affluence, which always, even so, contains built-in requirements for further improvements. We speak with amazement and admiration of the consumption miracle, conceiving of it as assuming ever larger proportions over the decades, without it having any counterpart in another miracle — that of complete material satisfaction.

The only book to achieve fame in recent years by questioning many of our current economic efforts is J. K. Galbraith's *The Affluent Society*. However, its influence on contemporary thought is not in proportion to its fame. The economists, at least, seem to be entirely unaffected by Galbraith's theses. This is probably because Galbraith based his argument more on intuition and aversion than on any analytical model. Among the professionals his work has come to be regarded as mere opinion in a saleable carton of attractive prose. The poverty of subsequent discussion on affluence emerges clearly in three articles where a well-known economist, Harry G. Johnson, has tried to deal with Galbraith's important book. After dissecting what should more appropriately be utilized as a stimulus to further thought, Johnson achieves the following winged words with their comforting conclusion in favor of the conventional wisdom: "The argument I have been presenting is concerned with the welfare problem raised by created wants, and leads to the comforting conclusion that the fact of want-creation does not invalidate the assumption that an increase in national income carries with it an increase in welfare."

"Futurology" the science or the art of making informed guesses about the future is much in vogue — and rightly so. This would suggest that analysis of ultimate economic matters would attract much attention which penetrates deeper than superficial extrapolations. Why has this not happened? The main reason must be that the analytical tools developed by economists are unsuitable for the creation of any eschatological system of thought in economics. Our economic analysis permits us only to visualize a general increase in welfare, without any internal tensions. It is also quite possible that the required analytical framework has not been erected, because people have been unwilling to clear the ground for thoughts that could lead to the conclusion that economic progress, by its own success, will eliminate the need for its continuation. The idea of progress — which means at present economic and technological progress — is, as J. Bury has pointed out, "the animating and controlling idea of western civilization." To protect ourselves against possible traumatic reflections, we avoid thoughts which may force us to admit that such progress is a temporary means, rather than an eternal goal. The validity of technological conquests even of a suicidal sort remains unquestioned. How then can we expect the validity of a much less dangerous process of economic growth to be questioned? Our vested interests in progress are too strong for that.

Under all circumstances, a time allocation theory offers new starting points for future economic research and for speculation on the economic future.

Partial Affluence

The visions of a general affluence are interesting, not only because they have failed to evoke discussion as to their own implications; they are also remarkable by virtue of their analytical imperfection. The forecasts of economists are misleading, because they relate only to the way in which one type of resources will develop. A time allocation theory offers new perspectives. This it does by drawing attention also to how the relative supply of time changes as the result of growth. As we knew, it is not only the absolute supply of one type of resources that is important; the *proportion* between the two main types of resources in the consumption process — time and goods — will also influence the content of development. To reiterate the main theme of this essay, affluence and scarcity are relative terms. Economic growth will not produce affluence in all respects. Affluence will be partial.

An increasing welfare in the form of an increasing volume of consumption goods will not produce an unproblematic increase in general well-being. That wealth does not guarantee happiness is no new discovery. What may be a new discovery, however, is that we can distinguish a mechanism, by which a rising volume of consumption itself causes a number of inner contradictions, which will affect our ultimate assessment of the results of our efforts toward growth.

As efforts to achieve growth accelerate during the period of decadence, the following phenomena will become increasingly noticeable. The extent to which we pay attention to them is a matter of personal choice. But we shall be obliged, inevitably, to reflect upon their meaning.

a. There will be an increasingly hectic tempo of life, marked by careful attempts to economize on increasingly scarce time.

b. There will be an expanding mass of goods, which will make great demands on time in the form of such maintenance and service tasks that cannot very well be mechanized. This will happen in spite of a decline in maintenance per item.

c. Since affluence is only partial, there will be increasing hardships for those whose welfare does not primarily require abundant goods but the scarce time of their fellow creatures. While the aged, in the beginning of the initial growth period, lacked bed and bread, they will towards the end of the period of growth mania lack a nurse.

d. There will be a curious combination of an increasing attachment to goods in general and, owing to a low degree of utilization and a rapid turnover, an increasing indifference to each of them in particular.

e. There will be a declining competitive position for time devoted to the cultivation of mind and spirit and for the time spent on certain bodily pleasures. *Dolce far niente.*

f. There will be a declining utility of income but not an exhaustion of wants; in order to achieve some addition to material well-being, increasing attention will, therefore, be given to further economic advances.

g. In the name of economic progress, there will be increasing emphasis on rational economic policies and behavior, but for this very reason also — as stated by the rationale of increasing irrationality — there will be a growing number of ill-considered decisions.

h. There will be a new form of economic "unfreedom," marked not by a fight for economic survival, but by an obsession with growth that sometimes forces us, in the name of registered increases in economic growth, to allocate our economic resources, including time itself, in destructive ways — to destroy God-given bases for life, i.e., air, water, earth, natural beauty, and our own heredity.

A Second Revolution of Rising Expectations

The underdeveloped world and its ancient ways of life are now torn by what has been called "a revolution of rising expectations." This revolution has been stirred by awareness among the leaders of an unnecessary poverty of goods. We should not denigrate the great results of that economic growth which has lifted the now affluent countries from a subsistence level. Yet we may ask ourselves whether some day in the future an awareness of the consequences of an increasing scarcity of time caused by continued economic growth will not set up a new kind of revolution of rising expectations. Certainly, a constant hunt to secure the basic necessities of life is presently regarded as a degrading existence. Perhaps being constantly chased by a scarcity of time will some day be recognized as an equally undignified way of life.

There is already a number of dissenters rejecting the values of the "consumption society." Michael Harrington, in discussing *The Other America,* devotes a certain amount of attention to the poor who have, for intellectual reasons, created their own poverty. "They accept the poverty because it provides them a certain freedom. As one writer brilliantly described them, they reject the working world because it does not give them time . . . perhaps it is more significant to remember that our affluent society contains those of talent and insight who are driven to prefer poverty, to choose it, rather than to submit to the desolation of an empty abundance."

How, if at all, the second revolution of rising expectations will come about and how that new society will function can only be guessed at. Its chief characteristic must be, however, that it requires a change at heart of the individual, rather than a change in the political system of the society. The regiment of consumption cannot be abolished collectively through political pressure. A society escaping from the decadence of growth can be formed only by a sum of individuals individually transformed. In Aldous Huxley's book *Island,* in which he tries to outline a better order of things, the individuals have chosen to construct their society in awareness of the conflict existing between continuous efforts to increase economic growth, as measured in volume of goods, and attempts to create "life before death."

. . ."Whereas *we*," said Dr. Roberts, "have always chosen to adapt our economy and technology to human beings — not our human beings to somebody else's economy and technology. We import what we can't make; but we make and import only what we can afford. And what we can afford is limited not merely by our supply of pounds and marks and dollars, but also and primarily (*primarily,* he insisted) by our wish to be happy, our ambition to become fully human.". . .

The literature of Utopia that tried to lead an age is now virtually dead. Utopias are rated impractical and meaningless — unfitted to promote the interests of economic progress to which we are committed. Yet Utopian inspiration and guidance is required to reformulate the purposes of all our progress.

The main arguments presented in this essay can be formalized within some simple mathematical models.

The effect of an increase in productivity on the allocation of time between work and nonwork activities

Assume we have a utility function

[1] $$U = f(Q, T_c)$$

where Q is the number of units of consumption goods and T_c the number of hours devoted to consumption purposes. The function is assumed to be twice differentiable and such that f_1 and f_2 are positive, f_{11} and f_{22} negative, and $f_{12} = f_{21}$ the-cross-derivatives positive.

We have two constraints to take into account

[2] $$Q = pT_w$$

and

[3] $$T = T_w + T_c$$

where p is a productivity index measuring the number of consumption goods earned per hour of work (T_w) and T is the total number of hours available per time period.

We now assume that individuals wish to maximize their utility (U). We can then form the following Lagrangean function:

[4] $$L = f(Q, T_c) + \lambda[Q - p(T - T_c)]$$

Differentiate this function with respect to Q, T_c and the multiplier λ. Put the partial derivatives equal to zero, as required by the first-order conditions for a maximum.

* I am greatly indebted to K.-G. Mäler who has helped me in my efforts to translate my thoughts into mathematical form. I also wish to thank Anders Holvid who has assisted me in the execution of a number of calculations. Mäler and Holvid are not responsible for whatever errors and inelegances may mark the exposition.

[5]
$$\frac{\partial L}{\partial Q} = f_1 + \lambda = 0$$

[6]
$$\frac{\partial L}{\partial T_c} = f_2 + \lambda p = 0$$

[7]
$$Q - p(T - T_c) = 0$$

In order to explore the second-order conditions, we form the bordered Hessian determinant:

$$D = \begin{vmatrix} 0 & 1 & p \\ 1 & f_{11} & f_{12} \\ p & f_{12} & f_{22} \end{vmatrix}$$

Expanding this determinant, we find that it is positive as required for a maximum.

Differentiate equations 5–7 with respect to p.

[8]
$$f_{11} \frac{dQ}{dp} + f_{12} \frac{dT_c}{dp} + \frac{d\lambda}{dp} = 0$$

[9]
$$f_{12} \frac{dQ}{dp} + f_{22} \frac{dT_c}{dp} + p \frac{d\lambda}{dp} = -\lambda$$

[10]
$$\frac{dQ}{dp} + p \frac{dT_c}{dp} = T - T_c$$

The determinant of this system is equal to the bordered Hessian, the sign of which we have already investigated. As $D \neq 0$, we can use Cramer's rule. We obtain

[11] $\quad \dfrac{dT_c}{dp} = \dfrac{1}{D} \begin{vmatrix} f_{11} & 0 & 1 \\ f_{12} & -\lambda & p \\ 1 & T - T_c & 0 \end{vmatrix} = \dfrac{1}{D} [\lambda - (T - T_c)(f_{11} p - f_{12})]$

From equation 5 we know that λ is negative. In accordance with the assumption made about the utility function, we also know that the second part of the bracket is positive. Thus the sign of the expression cannot be determined.

That work time may increase or fall as a result of a change in productivity is well known from economic theory. Thus what is usually referred to as "free time" may increase or decrease. What in fact happens will depend upon the relative strength of the income effect (a person can afford to get more leisure) and the substitution effect (leisure is more expensive in comparison with goods).

The effect of an increase in productivity on the volume of consumption goods

In order to find out how the volume of consumption will change, we may solve equations 8–10 for dQ/dp. We obtain

[12] $$\frac{dQ}{dp} = \frac{1}{D}\left[-p\lambda + (T - T_c)(pf_{12} - f_{22})\right]$$

This expression is positive. More Q will be consumed when p rises. This means among other things that T_c cannot increase so much (if it increases at all) that Q falls when p rises.

The effect of an increase in productivity on the commodity intensity of consumption time

To explore how the average consumption time per consumption goods changes when p changes, we make use of the formula for derivation of a quotient

[13] $$\frac{d\left(\dfrac{T_c}{Q}\right)}{dp} = \frac{Q\,\dfrac{dT_c}{dp} - T_c\,\dfrac{dQ}{dp}}{Q^2}$$

If we substitute equations 11 and 12 into this, we obtain

[14] $$\frac{d\left(\dfrac{T_c}{Q}\right)}{dp} = \frac{1}{Q^2 D}\left[Q\{\lambda + (T - T_c)(f_{12} - pf_{11})\} \right. $$
$$\left. - T_c\{-p\lambda + (T - T_c)(pf_{12} - f_{22})\}\right]$$

However, the sign of this expression cannot be determined without further assumptions. If we make the assumption that the utility function is homogenous of degree r we know that

$$f_{11}Q + f_{12}T_c = (r - 1)f_1$$
$$f_{12}Q + f_{22}T_c = (r - 1)f_2$$

Rearranging equation 14, we obtain

[14a] $$\frac{d\left(\dfrac{T_c}{Q}\right)}{dp} = \frac{1}{Q^2 D}\left[\lambda pT + (T - T_c)\{Qf_{12} + T_c f_{22} - p(Qf_{11} + T_c f_{12})\}\right]$$

We can now make use of the information we acquire from the assumption of a homogenous utility function. From the first-order maximum conditions we also know that $f_2 - pf_1 = 0$. This means that equation 14a can be reduced to

[14b]
$$\frac{d\left(\frac{T_c}{Q}\right)}{dp} = \frac{1}{Q^2 D} \lambda p T$$

This expression is negative. Consumption time per consumption goods will, under the assumptions made, decline when p rises. Thus the commodity intensity of the consumption process will increase. The assumption of a homogenous utility function means a considerable limitation, in comparison with the general utility functions which are usually introduced in utility theory. Yet it does not seem an unreasonable, and it is under all circumstances only a sufficient, and not a necessary, assumption for our conclusions to emerge. To determine how the commodity intensity of the consumption process changes when p changes must, however, in the final analysis be an empirical question. So far, all signs indicate that there has, in fact, been a gradual rise in the commodity intensity.

Reallocation of time between different consumption activities as a result of an increase in productivity

In order to explore how an increase in productivity affects the allocation of time between competing consumption activities, we shall formulate a model which distinguishes between two different activities. A fixed amount of consumption time $(\overline{T}_c)$ is to be allocated between T_{c1} and T_{c2}. The first activity is characterized by the fact that an average in Q into this activity does not raise the utility of T_{c1}. The second activity is of the usual type. We now get the following utility function:

[15] $$U = f(T_{c1}, T_{c2}, Q_2)$$

We have two budget constraints to take into account when maximizing U:

[16] $$p_1 \overline{Q}_1 + p_2 Q_2 = p(T - \overline{T}_c)$$

and

[17] $$T_{c1} + T_{c2} = \overline{T}_c$$

where p_1 and p_2 are prices of the two types of consumption goods.

We can now form the following Lagrangean function:

[18] $\quad L = f(T_{c1},\ T_{c2},\ Q_2) + \lambda[p_1\overline{Q}_1 + p_2 Q_2$
$$- p(T - \overline{T}_c)] + \mu(T_{c1} + T_{c2} - \overline{T}_c)$$

We differentiate L with respect to T_{c1}, T_{c2}, Q_2 and the two multipliers. The expressions so obtained are put equal to zero as required by first-order conditions for a maximum. The second-order conditions are assumed to hold. We then differentiate with respect to p. We get the following system of equations, written in matrix form:

[19]
$$
\begin{bmatrix}
f_{11} & f_{12} & f_{13} & 0 & 1 \\
f_{12} & f_{22} & f_{23} & 0 & 1 \\
f_{13} & f_{23} & f_{33} & p_2 & 0 \\
0 & 0 & p_2 & 0 & 0 \\
1 & 1 & 0 & 0 & 0
\end{bmatrix}
\begin{bmatrix}
\dfrac{dT_{c1}}{dp} \\[2mm]
\dfrac{dT_{c2}}{dp} \\[2mm]
\dfrac{dQ_2}{dp} \\[2mm]
\dfrac{d\lambda}{dp} \\[2mm]
\dfrac{d\mu}{dp}
\end{bmatrix}
=
\begin{bmatrix}
0 \\[2mm]
0 \\[2mm]
0 \\[2mm]
T_w \\[2mm]
0
\end{bmatrix}
$$

We now solve this system for dT_{c1}/dp and obtain

[20] $$\frac{dT_{c1}}{dp} = \frac{1}{D}\, p_2 T_w (f_{23} - f_{13})$$

Where T_w is work time, the determinant is negative. The whole expression is then negative if $f_{23} > f_{13}$, i.e., if an increase in Q_2 promotes the yield on time in the second activity more than in the first. This seems highly plausible. The first activity would then be "inferior," i.e., it would have a negative income elasticity.

Through this reallocation of time the marginal utility of consumption goods will decline less rapidly than otherwise. From equation 11 we know that the higher the marginal utility of consumption goods i.e., the lower λ lambda, the more likely it is that work time will not decline when p rises. Extensive reallocations of time of the sort we have discussed here may explain why, in the rich countries, the tendencies toward further reductions of work time have been fairly weak.

The reallocation of time between different activities will hurt, in particular, those pursuits which the original growth optimists hoped would attract a growing interest. Cultural pursuits belong to this group.

Equation 20 also provides a formalization of the increasing tempo of life that we may notice taking place. A slower tempo constitutes one way of spending time that, perhaps, is the best example of an activity, the yield of which cannot be increased through any addition of consumption goods. This is so by definition. "Peace and quiet" is thus an "inferior" way of passing time.

The effect of an increase in productivity on the volume of personal work

So far we have not distinguished between anything but work time and consumption time — although we have in the latter type of time included culture time and time used to adjust the speed of life. We shall now proceed to take into account that consumption goods make certain demands on personal work for maintenance tasks. The yield of a certain volume of consumption goods will then depend also on the amount of time spent on servicing these goods. We can specify the following utility function:

[21] $$U = f(R, T_c)$$

where R signifies real income determined in the following equation:

[22] $$R = g(Q, T_m)$$

where T_m is the amount of time in personal work. The g-function is assumed to be homogenous of the first degree. (The results which will be derived could be obtained without a limitation of the homogeneity to the first degree. However, assuming homogeneity of any degree makes the calculations somewhat more complicated.) We have the following budget constraints to take into account:

[23] $$Q = pT_w$$

and

[24] $$T = T_w + T_m + T_c$$

We can form the Lagrangean function:

[25] $$L = f(R, T_c) + \lambda[R - g(Q, T_m)] + \mu[Q - (T - T_c - T_m)p]$$

If we differentiate this function with respect to R, T_c, Q, T_m, and the two multipliers, we obtain a set of equations which can be equal to zero as required by first-order conditions for a maximum.

[26]
$$\frac{\partial L}{\partial R} = f_1 + \lambda = 0$$

[27]
$$\frac{\partial L}{\partial T_c} = f_2 + p\mu = 0$$

[28]
$$\frac{\partial L}{\partial Q} = -\lambda g_1 + \mu = 0$$

[29]
$$\frac{\partial L}{\partial T_m} = -\lambda g_2 + p\mu = 0$$

[30]
$$\frac{\partial L}{\partial \lambda} = R - g(Q, T_m) = 0$$

[31]
$$\frac{\partial L}{\partial \mu} = Q - (T - T_c - T_m)p = 0$$

Making use of equations 26 and 27, we can eliminate the multipliers. We get

[32]
$$f_1 g_1 - \frac{f_2}{p} = 0$$

[33]
$$f_1 g_2 - f_2 = 0$$

[34]
$$R - g(Q, T_m) = 0$$

[35]
$$Q - p(T - T_m - T_c) = 0$$

Replacing in equation 32 f_2 by $f_1 g_1$ (obtained from equation 33, we can write this equation $f_1 (pg_1 - g_2) = 0$. If f_1 at the maximum point is assumed to be positive, i.e., the constraints are binding, $(pg_1 - g_2)$ must be equal to zero. Equation 32 can then be written $pg_1 - g_2 = 0$. If we differentiate the system of equations that we now have with respect to p, we obtain the following system written in matrix form:

[36]
$$\begin{bmatrix} 1 & 0 & -g_2 & -g_1 \\ 0 & p & p & 1 \\ f_{11}g_2 - f_{12} & f_{12}g_2 - f_{22} & g_{22}f_1 & g_{12}f_1 \\ 0 & 0 & pg_{12} - g_{22} & pg_{11} - g_{12} \end{bmatrix} \begin{bmatrix} \dfrac{dR}{dp} \\[6pt] \dfrac{dT_c}{dp} \\[6pt] \dfrac{dT_m}{dp} \\[6pt] \dfrac{dQ}{dp} \end{bmatrix} = \begin{bmatrix} 0 \\ T_w \\ 0 \\ -g_1 \end{bmatrix}$$

From our assumption that the *g*-function is homogenous we know that

$$Qg_{11} + T_m g_{12} = 0$$

$$Qg_{12} + T_m g_{22} = 0$$

If we divide by T_w, replace Q/T_w with p, and introduce the letter a for T_m/T_w, we get

$$pg_{11} = -ag_{12}$$

$$pg_{12} = -ag_{22},$$

Furthermore, put

$$f_{11}g_2 - f_{12} = b \qquad (b < 0)$$

$$f_{12}g_2 - f_{22} = c \qquad (c > 0)$$

$$g_{22}f_1 \quad\;\; = d \qquad (d < 0)$$

$$\frac{g_1}{g_{22}(a+1)} = e \qquad (e < 0)$$

We also know that $pg_1 - g_2 = 0$, i.e., $pg_1 = g_2$. The system of equations 36 can now be written

$$[37] \cdot
\begin{bmatrix}
1 & 0 & -pg_1 & -g_1 \\
0 & p & p & 1 \\
b & c & d & -\dfrac{a}{p}d \\
0 & 0 & g_{22}(1+a) & g_{12}(1+a)
\end{bmatrix}
\begin{bmatrix}
\dfrac{dR}{dp} \\
\dfrac{dT_c}{dp} \\
\dfrac{dT_m}{dp} \\
\dfrac{dQ}{dp}
\end{bmatrix}
=
\begin{bmatrix}
0 \\
T_w \\
0 \\
g_1
\end{bmatrix}$$

If we divide the fourth row by $g_{22}(a+1)$, we obtain

$$[38]
\begin{bmatrix}
1 & 0 & -pg_1 & -g_1 \\
0 & p & p & 1 \\
b & c & d & -\dfrac{a}{d}d \\
0 & 0 & 1 & -\dfrac{a}{p}
\end{bmatrix}
\begin{bmatrix}
\dfrac{dR}{dp} \\
\dfrac{dT_c}{dp} \\
\dfrac{dT_m}{dp} \\
\dfrac{dQ}{dp}
\end{bmatrix}
=
\begin{bmatrix}
0 \\
T_w \\
0 \\
e
\end{bmatrix}$$

The determinant is positive, and — since it is not equal to zero — Cramer's rule can be applied.

If we investigate how the volume of personal work changes when p changes, we get

[39] $$\frac{dT_m}{dp} = \frac{1}{D}\left(- pebg_1 + ade + \frac{T_w ac}{p} + ce\right)$$

The sign of this expression cannot be determined. The time for personal work may rise or fall when p rises.

The effect of an increase in productivity on the quality of services

We are also interested in how the volume of personal work changes *per consumption product*, i.e., in $\dfrac{d\left(\dfrac{T_m}{Q}\right)}{dp}$.

If we first explore dQ/dp, we find that

[40] $$\frac{dQ}{dp} = \frac{1}{D}\left[pe(d + bpg_1) - pce + T_w c\right]$$

This expression is positive, i.e., Q will rise when p *rises*. According to the rules for differentiation of a quotient

$$\frac{d\left(\dfrac{T_m}{Q}\right)}{dp} = \frac{Q\dfrac{dT_m}{dp} - T_m \dfrac{dQ}{dp}}{Q_2}$$

If we introduce the expressions for dT_m/dp and dQ/dp into this formula and simplify, we obtain

[41] $$\frac{d\left(\dfrac{T_m}{Q}\right)}{dp} = \frac{g_1}{Qg_{22}(a + 1)};$$

This expression is negative. Under the assumptions made,* we would thus get a declining service quality in the form of a falling volume of personal work per consumption goods. This may happen simultaneously with an increase in the total volume of personal work. Thus there will be a decline of services in the service economy.

* It may be pointed out anew that the same result will be obtained, even if we assume a g-function which is homogenous of any degree rather than of degree one. Furthermore, the homogeneity assumption is sufficient, rather than necessary, and much more plausible in this case than in the case of utility functions.

CHAPTER I

The chapter quotation is from Michel Quoist, *Prayers of Life,* Logos Books, Gill and Son, Dublin and Melbourne, 1966, p. 76. Copyright 1963 by Sheed and Ward, Inc.

Walter Kerr's book *The Decline of Pleasure* was published by Simon and Schuster, New York, 1965. The quotation is from p. 39.

Two anthropological studies which explore differences in time attitudes in different cultures are those of Edward T. Hall, *The Silent Language,* Doubleday, New York, 1959; and Margaret Mead (ed.), *Cultural Patterns and Technical Change,* UNESCO, Paris, 1953. These and some more such studies are discussed in Chapter II. Studies in social anthropology which, on the other hand, do not seem to devote any attention at all to time attitudes are, for instance, S. F. Nadel, *The Foundations of Social Anthropology,* Cohen & West Ltd., London, 1951; Ralph Piddington, *An Introduction to Social Anthropology,* Oliver and Boyd, London, 1950; and G. Boalt, B. Hanssen, and L. Gustafsson, *Socialantropologi,* Natur och Kultur, Stockholm, 1960. The effects of opulence on the national character have been discussed by David M. Potter, *People of Plenty,* University of Chicago Press, Chicago & London, 1954.

As to sociological works on time budgets, the following may be mentioned: G. A. Lundberg, Mirra Komarovsky, and Mary A. McInerny, *Leisure: A Suburban Study,* Columbia University Press, New York, 1934; Pitirim A. Sorokin and Clarence Q. Berger, *Time-Budgets of Human Behavior,* Harvard University Press, Cambridge, Mass., 1939; Eric Larrabee and Rolf Meyersohn (eds.), *Mass Leisure,* The Free Press, Glencoe, Ill., 1958; Max Kaplan, *Leisure in America: A Social Inquiry,* John Wiley & Sons, New York, 1960; Sebastian de Grazia, *Of Time, Work, and Leisure,* Twentieth Century Fund, New York, 1962. For further studies it is possible to explore the wealth of references in de Grazia, *Of Time.* Also Reuel Denney and Mary Lea Meyersohn, "A Preliminary Bibliography on Leisure," *American Journal of Sociology,* May 1957, pp. 602–15. A sociological work with a clear statement of time as a scarce resource exposed to the economic principles of allocation is George Soule, *What Automation Does to Human Beings,* Sidgwick and Jackson, London, 1956, Ch. 6. On the methodological problems of making time budget studies, see Nelson N. Foote, "Methods for Study of Meaning of Use of

Time", in Robert W. Kleemeier (ed.), *Aging and Leisure,* Oxford University Press, New York, 1961, pp. 155–76.

The psychiatric study that discusses time problems is John Cohen, "Subjective Time," in J. T. Fraser (ed.), *The Voices of Time,* George Braziller, New York, 1966. The quotation is from p. 271. On the whole, this collection of essays on time makes fascinating reading.

For instance, John F. Due, *Intermediate Economic Analysis,* 3rd ed., Richard D. Irwin, Homewood, Ill., 1956, presents the labor-leisure time allocation theory that is standard in economic analysis. See pp. 328 ff. The statistical study relating income level and hours of work in various countries is Gordon C. Winston "An International Comparison of Income and Hours of Work," *Review of Economics and Statistics,* February 1966. The quotation is taken from p. 28. Many text books do not even bother to mention that the utility of a certain quantity of a product, say, a pound of coffee, depends upon the length of the period within which this quantity is to be consumed. See, however, Lloyd G. Reynolds, *Economics,* revised ed., Richard D. Irwin, Homewood, Ill., 1966, pp. 138–39; and J. M. Henderson and R. E. Quandt, *Microeconomic Theory,* International Student ed. McGraw-Hill and Kōgakusha, New York and Tokyo, 1958, p. 9. But perhaps other text book authors find this fact both self-evident and trivial.

The three papers which do introduce time as a resource in consumption are: Roy F. Harrod, (unnamed paper) in Committee for Economic Development, *Problems of United States Economic Development,* Vol. I (mimeo), January 1958, pp. 207–13; J. Mincer, "Market Prices, Opportunity Costs, and Income Effects," in *Measurement in Economics. Studies in Mathematical Economics and Econometrics in Memory of Yehuda Grunfeld,* Stanford University Press, Stanford, 1963; Gary S. Becker, "A Theory of the Allocation of Time," *Economic Journal,* September 1965, pp. 493–517.

It may be added that the concept of "time" figures extensively in economic analysis in a completely different sense from the one in which it is being used in this essay and by these three previous authors. Time is introduced as a dimension which sets up lags and expectations, and which permits the connection of casually related factors in a noninstantaneous manner. This time is a necessary ingredient in a process analysis undertaken to study paths towards an equilibrium (or away from an equilibrium). The concept of time in this essay is not the one which is introduced to conduct dynamic analysis. Time as introduced here is a resource of individuals, like any other resource. It has to be allocated according to certain principles, and these principles may very well be handled in static or comparative static analysis. Evidently, *changes* in this allocation may, if this is found convenient, be studied, also *overtime,* i.e., within the formal framework of dynamic analysis.

The reference to Veblen's gilded leisure class alludes to arguments presented in Thorstein Veblen, *The Theory of the Leisure Class,* Viking Press, New York, 1899.

The Ancient Greek concept of "leisure" is discussed, e.g., by S. de Grazia, *Of Time,* Ch. I. For a treatment of what is the "cultural" leisure problem in the U.S. and Soviet Union, see two papers by Paul Hollander, "Leisure as An American and Soviet Value," *Social Problems,* Fall 1966, pp. 179–88, and "The Uses of Leisure," *Survey — a Journal of Soviet and East European Studies,* July 1966, pp. 40–50.

CHAPTER II

The introductory quotation is from John Cohen, "Subjective Time," in J. T. Fraser (ed.), *The Voices of Time,* p. 272.

As to the concept of "disguised unemployment" see, for instance, Charles P. Kindleberger, *Economic Development,* second ed., McGraw-Hill, New York, 1965, p. 175; H. Myint, *The Economics of the Developing Countries,* Hutchinson University Library, London, 1964, pp. 86–90; and Gerald M. Meier (ed.), *Leading Issues in Development Economics,* Oxford University Press, New York, 1964, pp. 77–85.

That in the preindustrial era the number of holidays and holy days was surprisingly high is pointed out, for instance, by Ida Craven in her contribution on "Leisure" in *Encyclopaedia of the Social Sciences,* Macmillan, New York, 1933. The quotation is from p. 403. See also Karl-Gustaf Hildebrand, "Arbetstid, människovärde och produktivitet — ett historiskt perspektiv," in *Individen och Arbetstiden,* Studieförbundet Näringsliv och Samhälle, Stockholm, 1965, p. 11, and the concluding chapter in Hutton Webster, *Rest Days,* Macmillan, New York, 1916. For the same observation see also S. de Grazia, *Of Time,* p. 89. References to additional material in this work, p. 493.

In Margaret Mead, *Cultural Patterns,* pp. 75 and 179–80, there are references to the time attitudes of the Burmese and the Spanish-Americans in the Southwest of the United States. The quotation from Edward T. Hall is, *Silent Language,* p. 26. On the Nuer, see E. E. Evans-Pritchard, *The Nuer: A Description of the Modes of Livelihood and Political Institutions of a Nilotic People,* Clarendon Press, Oxford, 1940, p. 103. Reprinted by permission of Clarendon Press. "Concepts of Time among the Tiv of Nigeria," by Paul Bohannan is to be found in *Southwestern Journal of Anthropology,* Autumn 1953, pp. 251–62. Quotation from p. 262. On the lack of time concepts in poor societies, see also Charles C. Hughes, "The Concept and Use of Time in the Middle Years: The St. Lawrence Island Eskimos," in Robert W. Kleemeier (ed.), *Aging and Leisure,* Oxford University Press, New York, 1961, pp. 91–95.

The reference to Swedish time attitudes around the turn of the century is from Vilhelm Moberg, "Svensk sommar" in *Året i Norden,* Bonniers, Stockholm, 1962, p. 16.

The quotation describing the Greek concept of time is from Margaret Mead, *Cultural Patterns,* pp. 90–92. As to the Japanese time attitudes, see Robert J. Smith, "Japan: The Later Years of Life and The Concept of Time," in Kleemeier (ed.), *Aging and Leisure,* pp. 95–100. The quotation from Walter Kerr is, *Decline,* p. 40.

On the modern theory of the firm and organizational slacks, see Richard M. Cyert & James G. March, *A Behavioral Theory of the Firm,* Prentice-Hall, Englewood Cliffs, N. J., 1963, pp. 36–38, or Kalman J. Cohen & Richard M. Cyert, *Theory of the Firm,* Prentice-Hall, Englewood Cliffs, N. J., 1965, pp. 332–35.

The Swedish publishing company Almqvist & Wiksell has, it mgiht be mentioned, put out for advertising purposes a brochure on personal time budgeting (*Om personlig tidsplanering*). George Woodcock's point is made in his paper "The Tyranny of The Clock," *Politics magazine,* October 1944, reprinted in Arthur Naftalin a.o. (eds.), *An Introduction to Social Science,* Lippincott, Chicago, 1953, Part One, pp. 209–12.

J. R. Seeley, R. A. Sim, and E. W. Loosley, *Crestwood Heights,* John Wiley & Sons, New York, 1963. Excerpts are from pp. 63–74. Additional evidence of time consciousness in rich countries can be found in Max Kaplan, *Leisure,* 264–67; Edward T. Hall, *Silent Language,* Ch. 9; and Robert J. Smith, "Cultural Differences in The Life Cycle and The Concept of Time," in Robert W. Kleemeier, *Aging,* pp. 83–86. In this brief essay, the interesting point is also made that for old people the time situation changes drastically. "To an individual in his later years, this very concept of time may prove a marked depressant. Used to being active, he may now find that an absence of scheduling poses problems for him. It no longer matters much that he is on time for anything. He may, indeed, find that he is not required to arise at a certain hour or that he may eat at any time he chooses, in short, that his days are now stretches of time which an earlier discipline will not fill up" (pp. 85–86). Thus, for old people even in rich countries there is some involuntary idleness, or at least "organizational slack" which, because of previous life habits, might be difficult to adjust to.

The medical problems of stress are widely published. A summary of the influence of time sense — "time claustrophobia" — on mental patients can be found in Otto Fenichel, *The Psychoanalytic Theory of Neurosis,* Norton, New York, 1945. The effect of income on life expectancy is discussed in Ch. V in this book.

"In Praise of Idleness" can be found in the collection of essays, Bertrand Russell, *In Praise of Idleness,* Unwin Books, London, 1960. The quotation is from p. 18.

CHAPTER III

The opening quotation is from C. E. M. Joad, *Diogenes; or, The Future of Leisure* (in the series *Today and Tomorrow*), Kegan Paul, Trench & Trubner Co., London, 1928, p. 19.

The orginal piece on the labor-leisure allocation in economic theory is Lionel Robbins, "On the Elasticity of Demand for Income in Terms of Effort," *Economica,* June 1930, pp. 123–29. Richard A. Musgrave, *The Theory of Public Finance,* McGraw-Hill, New York, 1959, pp. 233–38 has a good discussion of the problem. See also J. M. Henderson and R. E. Quandt, *Microeconomic Theory,* pp. 23–24.

Arthur Lewis' paper is "Economic Development with Unlimited Supplies of Labour," *The Manchester School,* May, 1954.

There is a report from The Survey Research Center of the University of Michigan commenting on, among other things, the purchase of outside help by different income groups. See James N. Morgan, Ismail A. Sirageldin, and Nancy Baerwaldt, *Productive Americans,* Institute for Social Research, Ann Arbor, Mich., 1966, pp. 163–84.

Table 1 has been calculated using the following four equations:

$$T_w + T_m + T_c = T$$

$$T_{wp} = Q$$

$$T_m = Q_{tm}$$

$$T_c = Q_{tc}$$

where we have the following four variables: T_w = work time, T_m = maintenance time, $T_c =$ consumption time, and $Q =$ number of consumption goods. We have three constants: $T =$ total time assumed to be 16 hours per day, $t_m =$ average maintenance time per consumption item, and $t_c =$ average consumption time per product, both assumed in this numerical example to amount to ½ hour. Finally, we have one parameter: $p =$ the productivity level. We wish to study the effects of changes in this parameter. To see how work time is affected, for instance, we can solve the following equation obtained through substitution.

$$T_w + T_w p(t_m + t_c) = T$$

The derivative of T_w with respect to p is negative.

Table 2 is calculated from seven equations, namely,

$$T_{w1} + T_{w2} + T_m + T_c = T$$

$$T_{w1} p' = Q$$

$$T_c = Q t_c$$

$$T_m = \frac{1}{2} Q t_m$$

$$T_{w2} = \frac{1}{2} Q t_m \frac{p}{p'}$$

$R = Q + S$
$S = T_{w2} p'$

Tw_1 is the number of hours worked to obtain consumption goods to be used by the individual himself (Q) and T_{w2} is the number of hours worked to pay for services. The volume of such goods is denoted by S. The sum of Q and S is total production or R. We have in this case two parameters, namely, p' which is the productivity level of the individual himself and p which is the average productivity level. To see how T_{w1} is affected by changes in p' and (or) in p we can solve the following equation obtained through substitution

$$T_{w1} + \frac{1}{2} T_{w1} p' t_m \frac{p}{p'} + \frac{1}{2} T_{w1} p' t_m + T_{w1} p' t_c = T$$

The partial derivatives of T_{w1} with respect to p' and p are both negative, i.e., T_{w1} will decrease when p' or p rises. To see how T_{w2} is affected by changes in p' and (or) in p we can solve the following equation:

$$\frac{T_{w2}}{\frac{1}{2} t_m p} + T_{w2} + \frac{T_{w2} p'}{p} + \frac{T_{w2} p' t_c}{\frac{1}{2} t_m p} = T$$

The partial derivative of T_{w2} with respect to p' is negative, to read: p' with respect to p is positive.

CHAPTER IV

The opening quotation is from H. V. Routh, *Money, Morals and Manners as Revealed in Modern Literature,* Nicholson and Watson, London, 1935, p. 67.

The economics of the commercial service sector have during the last few years been given considerable attention by Victor R. Fuchs in particular. For instance, see his *Productivity Trends in the Goods and Service Sectors, 1929–61: A Preliminary Survey,* Occasional Paper 89, National Bureau of Economic Research, New York, 1964. Also by the same author *The Growing Importance of the Service Industries,* Occasional Paper 96, National Bureau of Economic Research, New York, 1965 (reprinted with minor changes from a paper in *The Journal of Business,* October 1965); "Output, Input, and Productivity in Selected Service Industries in the United States, 1939–1963," 9th General Conference of the International Association for Research in Income and Wealth, Lom, Norway, September 2nd–7th, 1965; "Growth of the Service Industries in the United States: A Model for Other Countries?" in *Manpower Problems in The Service Sector.* Papers for a Trade Union Seminar. Supplement to the report. International Seminars 1966:2. OECD, Paris, 1966, and *The Service Economy.* With the Assistance of Irving F. Leveson (mimeo.) National Bureau of Economic Research, New York, 1966.

On the same problem there is also a study by Maurice Lengellé, *The Growing Importance of the Service Sector in Member Countries,* OECD, Paris, 1966.

On the rate of technical progress in the service industry Fuchs concludes (Occasional Paper 96, p. 12): "That output per man grew much faster in goods than in services is clear beyond doubt, and that this differential largely or entirely accounts for the differential change in employment is also clear." In some service sectors there may even have been some technical retrogression. This may be the case, for instance, in the high-powered transportation sector. Reportedly, because of air and airport congestion, it took 42 minutes longer in 1965 to fly between

New York and Washington than it did in 1948. This is asserted in *The Economist*, July 24–30, 1965, p. 341. Lewis Herber, *Crises in Our Cities*, Prentice-Hall, Englewood Cliffs, N.J., 1965, cites information saying that vehicular progress in New York has dropped from 11.5 miles per hour in 1907 to 6 miles per hour in the jet era.

The somewhat surprising finding that families with more automatic home appliances do not seem to do less housework is taken from James N. Morgan, Ismail A. Sirageldin, and Nancy Baerwaldt, *Productive Americans*, pp. 111–12.

William J. Baumol has explored how employment in services and expenditures on services will change in relation to total employment and total expenditures under different assumptions as to the preference pattern, and under the assumption of slower technical progress in the service sector than in manufacturing. This he has done in his paper "Macroeconomics of Unbalanced Growth: The Anatomy of Urban Crisis," *American Economic Review*, June 1967, pp. 415–26.

The idea that Monday is required for people to recuperate from strenuous work and leisure activities over the week-end was advanced by V. W. Bladen in *Proceedings of the Ninth Annual Meeting of the Industrial Relations Research Associations,* Papers presented at Cleveland Ohio, December 28–29, 1956, p. 223.

CHAPTER V

The opening quotation is from Arnold J. Toynbee, *Change and Habit*, Oxford University Press, New York and London, 1966, p. 220.

Lebhar's attack on sleep is in the opening chapters of Godfrey M. Lebhar, *The Use of Time*, Chain Store, New York, 1958. The optimistic hope that the need for sleep will decrease substantially is voiced by Morris Ernst, *Utopia 1976*, Rinehart, New York, 1955, p. 14.

Besides frustrating attempts at cutting back hours of sleep to gain some hours for other pursuits, there may, of course, be some genuine technical progress in the regeneration of bodily and mental strength. Reportedly, the Russians are experimenting with a sleep machine called the "electrosone" which will pack a full night's sleep into just two hours or less. For this piece of information see Robert Lee, *Religion and Leisure in America,* Abingdon Press, New York, 1964, p. 19.

The *TV Guide for New Haven,* Conn., November 12–18, 1966, p. A-9 carried the advertisement for a germicide to eliminate the need for time-consuming vaginal douches. The statement about the "best dressed poverty" is to be found in Michael Harrington, *The Other America,* Penguin Books, Baltimore, Maryland, 1963, p. 12.

The following cook-books may be cited to show what is available to harried housewives: Peg Bracken, *I Hate to Cook Book,* Harcourt, New York, 1960; L. Langseth Christianssen, *The No Cooking Cookbook,* Coward, New York, 1962; Y. Y. Tarr, *The 10 Minute Cookbook,* Lyle Stuart, New York, 1965; and L. Langseth Christianssen, *The Instant Epicure Cookbook for Terribly Tired Gourmets,* Coward, New York, 1963. These books were found on the shelf of Macy's New Haven, in December 1966.

As to the problems of obesity and lack of exercise see, e.g., *Obesity and Health*: U.S. Department of Health, Education and Welfare, Public Health Service, Washington, 1966. The relationship between income and life expectancy is discussed by R. Auster, I. Leveson, and Deborah Sarachek, *The Production of Health, An Exploratory Study,* National Bureau of Economic Research, New York, December 1966 (mimeo.), and Victor R. Fuchs, "The Contribution of Health Services to the American Economy," *Milbank Memorial Fund Quarterly,* October 1966. The quotation is from p. 81.

The quotation from William H. Whyte, *The Organization Man,* about the conscience-ridden father, is from the Penguin edition, Harmondsworth, Middlesex, 1960, p. 140. The book which tries to sell itself as a guide to instant child upbringing is Marvin J. Gersch, *How to Raise Children at Home in Your Spare Time,* Stein and Day, New York, 1966. It was prominently advertised, for instance, in *The New York Times Book Review,* December 11, 1966. Evidently, it is also supposed to have a good market among harried intellectuals as it was also advertised in *The New York Review of Books,* April 20, 1967.

The relationship between family size and income has been widely discussed. The first work which tries systematically to introduce economic theory into this demographic problem is Gary S. Becker, "An Economic Analysis of Fertility," in *Demographic and Economic Change in Developed Countries,* National Bureau of Economic Research (Special Conference Series, 11), New York, 1960, pp. 209–31. J. Duesenberry stressed the time costs of children in his comments on Becker's paper. The ideas of Jacob Mincer on income and fertility are to be found in the paper already quoted many times. They are an application of his general argument that estimates of income elasticities will be biased when, parallell to the income changes, it is not taken into account that there must be price changes due to changes in the opportunity cost of time.

The police officer who has been quoted made his statement in *Svenska Dagbladet,* October 10, 1967. J. K. Galbraith, *The Affluent Society,* Hamish Hamilton, London, 1958, discusses the quality of public services.

The importance of non-interest costs in determining cash ratios is discussed by William J. Baumol, "The Transactions Demand for Cash: An Inventory Theoretic Approach," *Quarterly Journal of Economics,* November, 1952, pp. 545–56. See also J. Tobin, "The Interest-Elasticity of Transactions Demand for Cash," *Review of Economics and Statistics,* August 1956, pp. 241 – 47.

The selling suggestion that the two weeks before Christmas are the worst time of the year was made by shipping line in at least two advertisements, namely in the *New York Times* of October 17 and 23, 1966. The magnitude of the problem of disposal — the final service an item requires — is indicated by an assertion made in *Time Magazine,* November 18, 1966, p. 57. Here it was stated that the cost of disposing of the Sunday *New York Times* exceeds that of purchasing the paper — although in most cases the cost is borne by the individual.

CHAPTER VI

The opening quotation is from W. C. Mitchell, *The Backward Art of Spending Money and Other Essays,* McGraw-Hill, New York, 1937, p. 11.

Discussions of the rationality assumption in economic theory and criticism of this assumption from the psychologist's point of view can be found in the following works: Herbert A. Simon, "Theories of Decision-Making in Economics and Behavioral Science," *American Economic Review,* June 1959, pp. 253 – 83; James G. March and Herbert A. Simon, *Organizations,* John Wiley and Sons, New York, 1959; and Richard M. Cyert and James G. March, *A Behavioral Theory of the Firm,* Ch. 2.

Veblen's ridicule of the "economic man" can be found in "Why Is Economics Not An Evolutionary Science?" *Quarterly Journal of Econo-*

mics, 1898, reprinted in Veblen, *The Place of Science in Modern Civilization*, Russell and Russell, New York, 1961.

The economists' attempt to incorporate the costs of information in a study of allocation of resources can be found in the following papers: A. Charnes and W. W. Cooper, "The Theory of Search: Optimum Distribution of Search Effort," *Management Science*, October 1958, pp. 44–50; George J. Stigler, "The Economics of Information," *Journal of Political Economy*, June 1961, pp. 213–25; William J. Baumol and Richard E. Quandt, "Rules of Thumb and Optimally Imperfect Decisions," *American Economic Review*, March 1964, pp. 23–46; and Jacob Mincer, "Market Prices" in *Measurement in Economics*, pp. 79–81. The quotation from Stigler is from "Economics," p. 224.

The Canadian study of "impulse-buying" is C. John West, "Results of Two Years of Study into Impulse Buying," *The Journal of Marketing*, January 1951, pp. 362–63. The Du Pont studies are reported on in Hawkins Stern, "The Significance of Impulse Buying Today," *Journal of Marketing*, April 1962, pp. 59–62. Additional data on impulse buying can be found in *The Consumer's Food Buying Habits* by L. Moss, OECD, Paris, 1958. That housewives plan menus while shopping is asserted by Saul Nesbitt, "Today's Housewives Plan Menus as They Shop," *Nesbitt Associates Release*, New York, 1959, p. 2.

The Katona-Mueller study is by George Katona and Eva Mueller, "A Study of Purchase Decisions," in Lincoln H. Clark (ed.), *Consumer Behavior*, New York University Press, New York, 1955. The quotation is from p. 79. The findings presented in this report receive additional support from an ambitious Swedish study. See B. Wickström, *Konsumentens Märkesval* (Handelshögskolans i Göteborg skrifter 1965: 7), Gumperts, Göteborg, 1965.

That consumers often use price as an indicator of quality is stressed by Folke Ölander, "The Influence of Price on the Consumer's Evaluation of Products and Purchases" (mimeo.), The Economic Research Institute at the Stockholm School of Economics, Stockholm, 1966. The quotation is from p. 28. See this interesting paper for a wealth of references to additional studies in this area.

The text-book which actually refers to time pressures as a factor to take into account when considering marketing problems is John A. Howard, *Marketing Management*, rev. ed., Richard D. Irwin, Homewood, Ill., 1963, p. 93. This book also reports on various empirical facts of interest in the present context. See, for instance, p. 52.

The suggestion — in all likelihood erroneous for reasons advanced here — that advertising will become more and more directed toward the dissemination of information away from the provision of a rationale for choice is made by George Katona, *The Mass Consumption Society*, McGraw-Hill, New York, 1964, p. 296.

Data on the growth of advertising volume can be found in *Survey of Current Business*, U.S. Department of Commerce, current issues. For back references see the same source, Annual Supplements 1942, p. 29 and 1965, p. 54.

That the average American is reached by some sixteen hundred advertisements each day is asserted in Dexter Masters, *The Intelligent Buyer and the Telltale Seller*, Alfred A. Knopf, New York, 1966, p. 136. The average annual intake of radio and TV commercials of some ten thousand is a figure given by David Ogilvy, *Confessions of An Advertising Man*, McClelland, Toronto, 1963, p. 123 in the Swedish edition.

The two schools on the baseness and greatness of advertising, respectively, can be said to be represented by J. K. Galbraith, *The Affluent Society;* and Katona, *The Mass Consumption Society.*

The description of the technicalities of our foodstuffs is from Masters, *The Intelligent Buyer*, p. 73.

Alec Cairncross' ideas concerning the household as a productive unit are put forward in his paper "Economic Schizophrenia," *Scottish Journal of Political Economy*, February 1958, pp. 15-21.

CHAPTER VII

The opening quotation is from Hjalmar Söderberg, *Doktor Glas*, Bonniers folkbibliotek, Stockholm, 1949, p. 111.

Disraeli's amorous pursuits have been charted, for instance, by W. F. Monypenny and G. E. Buckle, *The Life of Benjamin Disraeli, Earl of Beaconsfield*, John Murray, London, 1920, Vol. V, p. 238 et seq.

The gradual disappearance of the *cinq-à-sept* institution in France was mentioned to me by a beautiful lady who knew this, I was told, from a report printed in *Le Figaro* a few years ago.

The quotation from de Grazia is *Of Time*, p. 342.

The lives of executives' wives are dissected by W. Lloyd Warner and James C. Abegglen, "Successful Wives of Successful Executives," *Harvard Business Review*, March–April, 1956, pp. 64–70. The quotation is from p. 65.

The report on the love life of Stockholm students is in *Gaudeamus*, September 9, 1966.

Time Magazine of August 19, 1966, pp. 40–42, has a write-up on the effects of the blackout of New York on nativity rates. The Chicago figure is from *New York Herald Tribune,* International Edition, October 17, 1967, p. 12.

The quotation is from Ovid's "Remedies of Love" lines 143 and 144. (Ovid, *The Art of Love and Other Poems.* With an English translation by J. H. Mozley. William Heinemann, London, 1947.) The passage from Charles Baudelaire is from "Le peintre de la vie moderne" in his *Oeuvres Complètes,* Vol. 2 (*L'Art Romantique*), Louis Conard, Paris, 1925, p. 88.

The present-day marriage manuals are characterized by Davis Riesman, *The Lonely Crowd,* Yale University Press, New Haven and London, 1961, p. 147. The "Sex is Dead" article is by Earl H. Brill and was carried by *The Christian Century* for August 3, 1966, pp. 957–59.

The quotation is from Walter Kerr's *The Decline of Pleasure,* p. 136. The comment by Erich Fromm is from his book, *The Art of Loving,* Harper & Row, Bantam Books, New York, 1963, p. 92.

CHAPTER VIII

The opening quotation is from an interview with Alberto Moravia in *La Tribune de Genève,* September 9–10, 1967.

For a discussion of the background of "leisure" as a concept denoting time for the cultivation of mind and spirit, see S. de Grazia, *Of Time,* Ch. 1 and an essay by Ida Craven under "Leisure" in *Encyclopaedia of the Social Sciences.* The quotation from Tibor Scitovsky is taken from his essay "What Price Economic Progress?" published in his book *Papers on Welfare and Growth,* Allen & Unwin, London, 1964, p. 209.

Aldous Huxley's comment on the cultural optimism is to be found in his book *Along the Road,* Chatto and Windus, London 1925, pp. 234–35.

The poem on unspoiled, low-keyed meditative pleasures is by Marya Mannes in *The Reporter* for July 5, 1962, p. 6. Copyright 1962 by The Reporter Magazine Co. Reprinted by permission of Harald Ober Associates Co. It is reproduced from Robert Lee, *Religion and Leisure in America,* p. 261.

Much of the empirical material in this chapter is from William J. Baumol and William G. Bowen, *Performing Arts: The Economic Dilemma,* Twentieth Century Fund, New York, 1966. Figure on audience composition can be found in this work, table IV–1, pp. 75–76. The analysis of sales of classical records is from p. 4, footnote 2. The analysis of expenditure data in the performing arts is from Ch. 3. The quotation made in this context is taken from p. 45. A study like the Baumol-Bowen one, but on Swedish conditions is under preparation by Harald Swedner. The references in the text are from his Ch. 3 (mimeo.).

The "practical curriculum" is discussed by William H. Whyte, *The Organization Man*, Ch. 7. The quotation (later on in this chapter) as to the reading habits, or nonreading habits, of the executive class is from pp. 141–42. Erich Fromm's views on the lash of concentration in our culture are expressed in *The Art of Loving*. The quotation is from p. 91. The quotation from Walter Kerr is from his *The Decline of Pleasure*, p. 22.

E. W. Martin, *The Standard of Living in 1860*, University of Chicago Press, Chicago, 1942, pp. 357–58 describes cultural life at the time. Copyright 1942 by The University of Chicago Press. Used with permission of The University of Chicago Press. So does Walter Kerr in *Decline*, pp. 66–86.

As to the Mexican aspirations, see Dr. Manuel German Parre, *El Nuevo Programa de Accion del PRI* (mimeo.), point 28, p. 13.

The quotation on culture in the mid-eighties is from Sir Herbert Read, "Atrophied Muscles and Empty Art," in Nigel Calder (ed.), *The World in 1984*, Vol. 2, Penguin Books, Harmondsworth, Middlesex, 1965, p. 92. For data on U.S. publishing see *Statistical Abstract of the United States*, Washington, e.g. 1965, pp. 526–27. As to Sweden, see the annual catalogue of the Bibliographical Institute of the Royal Library, Stockholm. In Sweden the number of new books published rose from four thousand in 1960 to fifty-five hundred in 1966.

Library circulation might be a better guide in evaluating how much people actually read. The index of American Public Library circulation increased by forty-six per cent from 1939 to 1964. Total population increased during this period by the same percentage. If we look at the composition of borrowers, we shall see that over this period total borrowing by adults has remained constant, which thus means a sharp decline in borrowings per capita. This decline is concentrated on fiction. See *American Library Association Bulletin*, May 1962, p. 474, and May 1965, p. 401. The significance of these data must not be overvalued, as much may be explained in terms of people at higher incomes preferring to buy rather than to borrow.

The quotation from George Katona is from his *The Mass Consumption Society*, pp. 66–67. Copyright 1964 by McGraw-Hill Book Co. Used with permission of McGraw-Hill Book Co.

As to statistics on admissions to legitimate theatre, etc., see U.S. Department of Commerce, *Survey of Current Business,* current issues.

The cultural boom is heralded in Arnold Mitchell and Mary Lou Anderson, *The Arts and Business,* Long Range Planning Report No. 140, Stanford Research Institute, Menlo Park, Calif., 1962. See also Lawrence C. Murdoch, Jr. "S.R.O. and SOS.: The Performing Arts Paradox," *Business Review,* Federal Reserve Bank of Philadelphia, March 1962, pp. 3–14; and Alvin Toffler, *The Culture Consumers,* St. Martin's Press, New York, 1964.

On the expansion of amateur art activity see, for instance, Rockefeller Panel Report, *The Performing Arts; Problems and Prospects,* McGraw-Hill, New York, 1965. As to the number of symphony orchestras, see *Statistical Abstract for the United States,* 1966, U.S. Bureau of the Census, Washington, table 300, p. 211. Statistics on museums can be found in *Statistical Abstract for the United States,* 1966, table 299, p. 211.

The statistical basis of the religious revival in the United States has been scrutinized in Charles Y. Glock and Rodney Stark, *Religion and Society in Tension,* Rand McNally, Chicago, 1965, Ch. 4. The reduction in social activities of the churches is reported on by W. W. Schroeder and V. Obenhaus, *Religion in American Culture,* The Free Press of Glencoe, New York, 1964, p. 43.

The information on Reform Judaism was given me in a letter from Gary S. Becker. For advertisements about the appropriate shortness of religious services for modern people, see, for instance, *Svenska Dagbladet,* March 23 and December 2, 1967. The quotations on religious life in *Crestwood Heights* are from J. R. Seeley, R. A. Sim, and E. W. Loosley, pp. 65–66.

CHAPTER IX

The opening quotation is from J. O. Wallin, "Tidens värde" in *Samlade Vitterhets-arbeten,* 5:e uppl., II delen, Adolf Bonnier, Stockholm, 1863, p. 190.

A survey of the various savings theories can be found in R. Ferber, "Research on Household Behavior," *American Economic Review,* March 1962, pp. 19–63. See also J. Tobin, "The Consumption Function" (mimeo.), extended version of an article prepared for the *International*

Encyclopedia of the Social Sciences, Macmillan, New York, published in 1968. The original contribution on what has come to be known as the "absolute income hypothesis" is J. M. Keynes, *The General Theory of Employment, Interest, and Money,* Harcourt, New York, 1936. It has been elaborated by J. Tobin, "Relative Income, Absolute Income, and Saving," in *Money, Trade, and Economic Growth. Essays in Honor of John Henry Williams,* Macmillan, New York, 1951, pp. 135–56. The first variant of the relative income hypothesis can be found in Dorothy S. Brady and Rose Friedman, "Savings and the Income Distribution," in *Studies in Income and Wealth,* vol. 10, National Bureau of Economic Research, New York, 1947, pp. 247–65. It was extended by J. Duesenberry, *Income, Saving, and the Theory of Consumer Behavior,* Harvard University Press, Cambridge, Mass., 1949. The life-cycle income hypothesis was first presented by F. Modigliani and R. Brumberg, "Utility Analysis and the Consumption Function," in K. K. Kurihara (ed.), *Post-Keynesian Economics,* Rutger University Press, New Brunswick, 1954. It has been reworked by A. Ando and F. Modigliani, "The 'Life-Cycle' Hypothesis of Saving," *American Economic Review,* March 1963, pp. 55–84. The better-known variant, the "permanent income hypothesis," is formulated by Milton S. Friedman, *A Theory of the Consumption Function,* National Bureau of Economic Research, Princeton University Press, Princeton, 1957.

Gary Becker has applied the time allocation approach to the savings problem in a recent mimeographed paper "The Allocation of Time and Goods Over Time," June 1967.

Economic theory discussions of the effects of taxes on work effort can be found in Richard A. Musgrave, *The Theory of Public Finance,* Ch. 11. Also Earl R. Rolph and George F. Break, *Public Finance,* Ronald Press, New York, 1961, pp. 151–57; R. Barlow and G. R. Sparks, "A Note on Progression and Leisure," *American Economic Review,* June 1964, pp. 372–77, and J. G. Head, "A Note on Progression and Leisure: Comment," *American Economic Review,* March 1966, pp. 172–79.

The most recent empirical study of the effects of taxes on the work effect of high income earners is Robin Barlow, Harvey E. Brazer, and James N. Morgan, *Economic Behavior of the Affluent,* The Brookings Institution, Washington, 1966, Ch. 10. References to other such studies may be found in this book. See footnote references on pp. 130–31.

CHAPTER X

The opening quotation is from J. M. Keynes, "Economic Possibilities for Our Grandchildren," in his *Essays in Persuasion,* Macmillan, London, 1931, p. 372.

For a survey of the secular stagnation doctrine, see Benjamin Higgins, "Concepts and Criteria of Secular Stagnation," in Lloyd A. Metzler and others (eds.) *Income, Employment and Public Policy, Essays in Honor of Alvin H. Hansen,* W. W. Norton & Co., New York, 1948, p. 82–107.

The two great Utopian studies referred to are Sir Thomas More, *Utopia,* ed. by Edward Surtz, Yale University Press, New Haven and London, 1964; and E. Bellamy, *Looking Backward, 2000–1887,* Houghton Mifflin, New York, 1929.

John Stuart Mill's chapter on the stagnant state is in his *Principles of Political Economy,* Longmans, Green and Co., London, 1909, Book IV, Ch. VI:2.

For the views of J. K. Galbraith on the saturation of material wants, see *The Affluent Society,* Chs. 10 and 11.

Roy F. Harrod presented his unusual diagnosis of the likelihood of a consumption maximum in a collection of essays, published by the Committee for Economic Development, *Problems of United States Economic Development* (mimeo.), vol. 1, January 1958, pp. 207–13.

The reference to the Veblen leisure class is, of course, a reference to the idle rich analyzed by Thorstein Veblen in his famous book *The Theory of the Leisure Class.*

"The miracle of consumption" is a phrase used by George Katona in *The Mass Consumption Society,* p. 9.

The article by J. S. Chapman was originally published in *Economic Journal,* March 1913, and is reprinted in *Readings in the Economics of Taxation,* selected by a Committee of The American Economic Association. Richard D. Irwin, Homewood, Ill., 1959.

CHAPTER XI

The opening quotation is from W. Bagehot, *Economic Studies,* 7th ed., Longmans, Green and Co., London, 1908, p. 202.

The quotation on growth urgency in the U.S. is from Moses Abramovitz, " Economic Growth in the United States," *American Economic Review,* September 1962, p. 762.

T. Wilson has discussed the possible explanations of the growing interest in growth. See his "The Price of Growth," *Economic Journal,* December 1963, pp. 603–17. E. J. Mishan has sharply criticized the current "growthmania." See his book *The Cost of Economic Growth,* Staples Press Ltd., London, 1967.

That we need to pursue economic growth to keep us from worse pursuits is a point made by J. M. Keynes, *The General Theory of Employment, Interest, and Money,* p. 374.

Data on average weekly hours in *Employment and Earnings Statistics for the United States,* 1909–60, Bulletin No. 1312, U.S. Department of Labor, Washington, 1961. For old data see J. F. Dewhurst and Associates, *America's Needs and Resources: A New Survey,* Twentieth Century Fund, New York, 1955, Appendix 20–4, p. 1073. For recent data, successive issues of *Monthly Labor Review.* For definition of "average work week" and methods of calculation, see U.S. Bureau of Labor Statistics, Department of Labor, "Techniques of Preparing Major BLS Statistical Series," *Bulletin 1168,* December 1954. For sample data on individual work weeks, see publications by the Census Bureau, *Current Population Reports,* Washington. For two useful analyses of the data, see Joseph S. Zeisel, "The Workweek in American Industry, 1850–1956," *Monthly Labor Review,* January 1958, pp. 23–29, reprinted in E. Larrabee and R. Meyersohn (eds.), *Mass Leisure;* Peter Henle, "Leisure and the Long Workweek," *Monthly Labor Review,* July 1966; and Forrest A. Bogan and Thomas A. Swanstrom, "Multiple Jobholders in May 1965," *Monthly Labor Review,* February 1966.

The National Association of Secondary-School Principals devoted the November 1965 issue of its *Bulletin* to the question of furthering economic studies. This matter is also discussed by C. W. McKee and H. G. Moulton, *A Survey of Economic Education,* The Brookings Institution, Washington, 1951.

F. A. von Hayek, *The Road to Serfdom,* University of Chicago Press, Chicago, 1944; R. Carson, *The Silent Spring,* Houghton Mifflin, New York, 1962.

The statement by Professor Neiburger is recorded by *The New York Times,* April 9, 1965.

A critical and well-informed review of the sufferings of various disabled minorities in the welfare state of Sweden is provided by Gunnar Inghe and Maj-Britt Inghe, *Den ofärdiga välfärden,* Tidens förlag, Stockholm, 1967.

CHAPTER XII

The opening quotation is from Thomas Carlyle, *Past and Present,* second ed., Chapman and Hall, London, 1845, p. 208.

Progress is characterized as the "animating and controlling idea of western civilization" by J. Bury in the Preface to his book *The Idea of Progress,* Macmillan, London, 1924. On the interesting subject of the notion of progress and present uncertainties as to its validity, see the introductory essay by George H. Hildebrand in *The Idea of Progress, A Collection of Readings,* selected by Frederick J. Teggart and revised by Hildebrand, University of California Press, Berkeley and Los Angeles, 1949.

The only study which in an ambitious fashion addresses itself to the problem of what the end-state of economic growth may look like is P. J. D. Wiles, *The Political Economy of Communism,* Basil Blackwell, London, 1962. The two last chapters in this book deal with the eschatology approach of capitalist rather than communist economies. Usually, books on the "future" are just more or less imaginative accounts of what now-known technologies, when brought out from the laboratory, will bring us in the way of new products and new ways of life. This approach is not really very helpful.

The papers by Harry G. Johnson in which he takes up Galbraith's criticism of our version of affluence are "The Consumer and Madison Avenue," *Current Economic Comment,* August 1960, pp. 3–10; "The Political Economy of Opulence," *Canadian Journal of Economics and Political Science,* November 1960, pp. 552–64, and "The Social Policy of an Opulent Society," in his collection of essays *Money, Trade and*

Economic Growth, Harvard University Press, Cambridge, Mass., 1962. The second paper is reprinted in this volume. The quotation is from the first paper, p. 9.

The quotation is from Aldous Huxley, *Island*, Chatto and Windus, London, 1962, p. 141.

The intellectuals living under self-chosen poverty are referred to by Michael Harrington in *The Other America*. The quotation is from pp. 87–88.